Brazilian

Amazon

Alex & Gardênia Robinson

Credits

Footprint credits

Editor: Alan Murphy
Maps: Kevin Feeney

Managing Director: Andy Riddle
Content Director: Patrick Dawson
Publisher: Alan Murphy
Publishing Managers: Felicity Laughton,
Jo Williams, Nicola Gibbs
Marketing and Partnerships Director:
Liz Harper
Marketing Executive: Liz Eyles
Trade Product Manager: Diane McEntee
Accounts Managers: Paul Bew, Tania Ross
Advertising: Renu Sibal, Elizabeth Taylor
Trade Product Co-ordinator: Kirsty Holmes

Photography credits

Front cover: Dreamstime
Back cover: Dreamstime

Printed in Great Britain by CPI Antony Rowe,
Chippenham, Wiltshire

Every effort has been made to ensure that
the facts in this guidebook are accurate.
However, travellers should still obtain
advice from consulates, airlines etc about
travel and visa requirements before travelling.
The authors and publishers cannot accept
responsibility for any loss, injury or
inconvenience however caused.

Publishing information

Footprint *Focus Brazilian Amazon*
1st edition
© Footprint Handbooks Ltd
May 2012

ISBN: 978 1 908206 65 7
CIP DATA: A catalogue record for this book
is available from the British Library

® Footprint Handbooks and the Footprint
mark are a registered trademark of Footprint
Handbooks Ltd

Published by Footprint
6 Riverside Court
Lower Bristol Road
Bath BA2 3DZ, UK
T +44 (0)1225 469141
F +44 (0)1225 469461
footprinttravelguides.com

Distributed in the USA by Globe Pequot Press,
Guilford, Connecticut

The content of Footprint *Focus Brazilian
Amazon* has been taken directly from
Footprint's *Brazil Handbook*, which was
researched and written by Alex and Gardênia
Robinson.

Contents

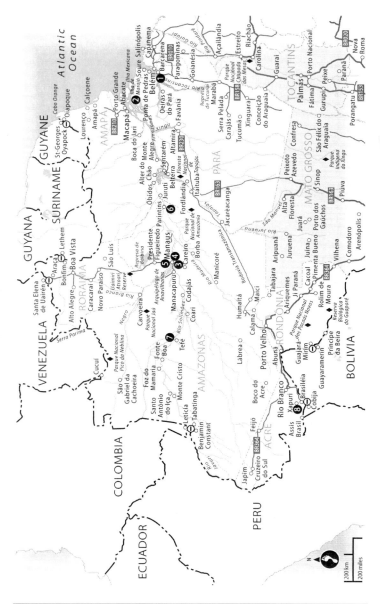

The Amazon is far more than a river. It is a continent of forests, savannahs and mountains, coursed by myriad veins of flowing water, pocked with lakes, overflowing with flooded forests and home to several million people. The wildlife is spectacular but the forests are dense and animals are far easier to spot in the Pantanal or cerrado. What is magical about the Amazon are its vast landscapes – its oceanic rivers, shimmering skies and labyrinthine backwaters – and the unique human drama which is played out here day after day.

The Amazon offers great diveristy. In the north, along the border with Venezuela and Colombia, are the forests and savannahs of the Guiana Shield where vegetation grows like a giant filigree over white sand and recycles 99.9% of its water and nutrients. West of here, the magnificent Rio Negro, black as coffee and fringed with pearly beaches, gushes past giant boulders the size of mountains before winding through the world's largest river archipelago, the Anavilhanas, and spreading out over several kilometres as it reaches the teeming port of Manaus.

In the east, the Amazon is joined by a series of rivers which are in their own right some of the largest in the world: the glassy blue Tapajos, the inky Xingu and, just as the river reaches its mouth, the Tocantins. Here the Amazon divides around an island the size of Denmark, the Ilha de Marajó, before spilling into the Atlantic, turning it fresh 100 miles offshore. Two cities lie on its banks: sleepy Macapá, with road connections to the Guianas; and bustling Belém, a historic colonial city with some of the best nightlife and cuisine in Brazil.

In the far west, the forests are gentler, more fertile and filled with life. Deforestation has been minimal and many tribal people remain uncontacted. The floating Uakari lodge is one of the Amazon's best.

In the southern Amazon state of Rondônia, the trees are broken by giant soya fields and cattle pasture, which cut into the green with geometric order. The state of Acre is far wilder and offers the chance to stay in indigenous villages or explore the forests around Xapuri – protected thanks to the world's first eco-martyr, Chico Mendes.

Planning your trip

When to visit the Brazilian Amazon

The best time for a visit is from April to June, and August to October. Business visitors should avoid mid-December to the end of February, when it is hot and people are on holiday. In these months, hotels, beaches and transport tend to be very crowded. July is a school holiday month. If visiting tourist centres such as Salvador, Rio and the colonial cities in Minas Gerais in the low season, be aware that some tourist sights may be closed.

In Rio de Janeiro conditions during the winter (May to September) are like those of a north European summer, including periods of rain and overcast skies, with temperatures from 14°C to the high 20s. It is more like a Mediterranean autumn in São Paulo and the southern states and it can get very cold in the far south; warm clothing is required as temperatures can change dramatically and it can get cold on high ground anywhere in Brazil, particularly at night. The heaviest rain is from November to March in Rio and São Paulo, and from April to August around Recife (although irregular rainfall causes severe draughts here). The rainy season in the north and Amazônia can begin in December and is heaviest from March to May, but it is getting steadily shorter, possibly as a result of deforestation. Few places get more than 2 m – the coast north of Belém, some of the Amazon Basin, and a small area of the Serra do Mar between Santos and São Paulo, where the downpour has been harnessed to generate electricity. Summer conditions all over the country are tropical, although temperatures rarely reach 40°C.

The average annual temperature increases steadily from south to north, but even on the equator, in the Amazon Basin, the average temperature is not more than 27°C. The highest recorded was 42°C, in the dry northeastern states. From the latitude of Recife south to Rio, the mean temperature is 23-27°C along the coast, and 18-21°C in the highlands. South of Rio, towards the boundary with Uruguay, the mean temperature is 17-19°C. Humidity is relatively high in Brazil, particularly along the coast. The luminosity is also very high, and sunglasses are advisable.

Getting to the Brazilian Amazon

There are a number of entrance points to the Amazon: **Manaus**, a city of 1.5 million people in the middle of the Amazon Basin, is the best place to organize safari cruises and lodges. It also offers the best access (by boat or air) to smaller towns further into the forest, such as Tefé. This is where one of the best Amazon rainforest lodges lies: **Mamirauá Ecological Reserve**, see page 84. Manaus is also the point of departure for a string of jungle lodges within a few hours of the capital – the best of which offer fascinating glimpses of both the forest and a timeless way of life – through some of the best community tourism projects in Brazil. It is also the jumping off point for the waterfalls of **Presidente Figueiredo** (see page 83), and the **Boi Bumba** festival in Parintins (see page 85).

Belém, at the mouth of the Amazon, began as a colonial slaving port and grew into a city with one of the best alternative cultural scenes in the north of Brazil. There are no forest lodges near Belém but it is possible to visit the rainforest on a cruise, with a small operator,

Don't miss ...

The numbers here relate to numbers on map on page 4.

or whilst staying on one of the river islands, such as **Marajó**. It is also possible to visit the forest from **Santarém**, a small city at the meeting of the Tapajós river and the Amazon.

Acre, in the south, is rapidly emerging as an alternative entrance point. The state lies right on the border with Peru and is served by regular flights and buses from Cuzco. **Xapuri**, which was the home of the first eco-martyr Chico Mendes (see box, page 113) is now the entrance point to the **Reserva Extrativista Chico Mendes** – a sustainable reserve where it is possible to see rubber tappers at work, and where there is abundant wildlife. Tour operator **Maanaim Amazônia**, see page 116, runs tours throughout Acre, including to indigenous villages far off the beaten track.

International flights into the Amazon Flights from the USA or Europe tend to come via Fortaleza, Rio de Janeiro, São Paulo or Salvador, with airlines such as TAP, www.flytap.com. Make sure you arrive two hours before international flights. It is wise to reconfirm your flight as departure times may have changed. ▶▶ *For airport tax, see page 20.*

Prices are cheapest in October, November and after Carnaval and at their highest in the European summer and the Brazilian high seasons (generally 15 December to 15 January, the Thursday before Carnaval to the Saturday after Carnaval, and 15 June to 15 August).

To **Manaus** from Miami with **TAM**, www.tam.com.br; from Panama (with connections onward to cities in Central America and the USA) with **Copa**, www.copaair.com; from Atlanta with **Delta**, www.delta.com.

To **Belém** from Haiti and Martinique via Cayenne (Guyane) with **Air Caribes**, www.aircaraibes.com, with connections from Paris; from Georgetown (Guyana) and Paramaribo (Suriname) with **META**, www.voemeta.com; from Paramaribo with **Surinan**.

To **Boa Vista** in Roraiama from Georgetown and Paramaribo with **META**.

To **Rio Branco** in Acre from Lima and Cuzco with **Star Peru**, www.starperu.com.

To **Cruzeiro do Sul** in Acre from Pucallpa in Peru with **Star Peru**, www.starperu.com.

Destinations in Colombia can be reached through **Leticia**, which is conjoined with Tabatinga on the far western Amazonian border.

International borders The Brazilian Amazon has a number of borders permitting overland or river crossings.

Venezuela can be reached from Boa Vista (Roraima) via Santa Elena, from where there are buses to Caracas; or with far more difficulty from São Gabriel da Cachoeira (Amazonas) via Cucuí (Amazonas) and San Carlos de Río Negro in Venezuela for Puerto Ayacucho, which also has buses to Caracas and the rest of the country.

Peru can be reached easily from Rio Branco in Acre with daily buses to Puerto Maldonado (via Assis Brasil and Iñapari in Peru), for onward land connections to Cusco. There are also numerous *combis* running between Assis Brasil and Iñapari. Peru can also be reached from Tabatinga or Benjamin Constant (Amazonas), from where there are boats running to Iquitos in Peru and onward boats to Pucallpa or flights to Lima.

Bolivia is reached from Guajará-Mirim (Rondônia), from where launches cross the river to Guayará Merin in Bolivia for buses to Rurrenabaque and La Paz. There are also connections from Rio Branco in Acre, via the border town of Brasiléia to Cobija in Peru, from where there are flights to La Paz and buses in the dry season.

Colombia is easily reached from Tabatinga (Amazonas) which is twinned and contiguous with the Colombian city of Leticia, from where there are flights to Bogotá.

Guyane (French Guiana) can be reached from Macapá (Amapá) by bus to Oiapoque, from where there are onward *combis* to St Georges Oyapock (Guyane), onward to Cayenne and all the way through Suriname to Guyana.

Guyana is easily reached by bus from Boa Vista via Bonfim (Roraima) to Lethem (Guyana), from where there are buses to Georgetown.

Transport in the Brazilian Amazon

By road

Aside from routes to Belém from the Atlantic Coast and from Tocantins, bus routes are limited to the following: **Amazonas/Roraima**: Manaus–Boa Vista (via Presidente Figuieredo), paved. **Roraima**: Boa Vista–Venezuela, paved. Boa Vista– Guyana, paved. **Amazonas**: São Gabriel da Cachoeira–Cucuí, paved and dirt. **Amapá**: Macapá–Oiapoque (from where there is boat and road access to French Guiana), dirt. **Pará**: Santarém–Cuiabá (in the Pantanal) is being improved and buses now run intermittently along the route through Pará into Mato Grosso with changes at Itauba for Alta Floresta and the Rio Cristalino; enquire at the *rodoviára* in Cuiabá or Santarém for the latest details. **Amazonas/Rondônia**: Humaitá–Porto Velho. **Rondônia/Acre**: Porto Velho–Rio Branco with onward buses to Cruzeiro do Sul and to Peru and Bolivia via Assis Brasil and Brasiléia. There are services to Guajará-Mirim along a small branch road, paved and dirt. **Rondônia/Mato Grosso**: Porto Velho–Cuiabá and onwards to the rest of Brazil, paved. There are dirt roads Manaus–Porto Velho, and Santarém–Porto Velho. These were overgrown and impassable when this book went to press, but there are plans to re-pave the road between Manaus and Porto Velho for the 2014 World Cup.

By plane

Because of the size of the country, flying is often the most practical option and internal air services are highly developed. All state capitals and larger cities are linked with each other with services several times a day, and all national airlines offer excellent service. Recent deregulation of the airlines has greatly reduced prices on some routes and low-cost airlines offer fares that can often be as cheap as travelling by bus (when booked through the internet). Paying with an international credit card is not always possible online; but it is usually possible to buy an online ticket through a hotel, agency or willing friend without surcharge. Many of the smaller airlines go in and out of business sporadically. **GOL, Oceanair, TAM, TRIP/Total, Varig,** and **Webjet** operate the most extensive routes. Most of their websites (see below) provide full information, including a booking service, although not all are in English.

Flight networks within the Amazon are extensive. **Trip,** www.voetrip.com.br, have the largest Amazonian network, which includes Manaus–São Gabriel da Cachoeira via Barcelos, and Manaus– Tabatinga via Tefé. **Trip** also connect Manaus with Brasília, Cuiabá and Campo Grande and Alta Floresta with Brasília, Cuiabá and the rest of Brazil. **META,** www.voemeta.com, flies Belém–Boa Vista and Belém–Santarém. **Sete,** www.voesete. com.br, flies Belém to Brasília with stops in the Xingu in Mato Gross, and to a number of smaller towns. **TAM,** www.tam.com.br, links Alta Floresta, Altamira, Santarém and all the Amazon state capitals with the rest of Brazil. **GOL,** www.voegol.com.br, connects all of the Amazonian state capitals with the rest of Brazil. **Avianca,** www.avianca.com.br, links Porto Velho with São Paulo, Rio and other major cities in Brazil.

Flight schedules are constantly changing and routes frequently close and re-open. Check the airline websites for the latest details and for prices.

Air passes TAM and GOL offer a 21-day **Brazil Airpass**, which is valid on any TAM destination within Brazil. The price varies according to the number of flights taken and the international airline used to arrive in Brazil. They can only be bought outside Brazil. One to four flights start at around US$540, five flights start at US$680, six flights start at US$840, seven flights start at US$990, eight flights start at US$1120, and nine flights start at US$1259. The baggage allowance is the same as that permitted on their international flights. TAM and Gol also operate as part of the **Mercosur Airpass**, which is valid for Brazil, Argentina, Chile, Uruguay and Paraguay using local carriers. It is valid for any passenger with a return ticket to their country of origin, and must be bought with an international flight. The minimum stay is seven days, maximum 45 and at least two countries must be visited. The maximum number of flights is eight. Fares, worked out on a mileage basis, cost between US$295 and US$1195. Children pay a discounted rate, and under-threes pay 10% of the adult rate. Some of the carriers operate a blackout period between 15 December and 15 January.

By boat
River boats are the buses of the Amazon and serve an extensive network, connecting both major and minor settlements. You won't see a great deal from the deck, especially if travelling downstream, as the boats stay in the middle of the river to catch the current. Going upstream, you will see an endless line of trees broken by the occasional village. However, the atmosphere on board is lively. Food is served, usually consisting of meat, beans and rice (which is brown as it is cooked in river water) and there is often a bar serving drinks and snacks. The size and quality of the boats varies greatly. The best boats ply the busiest routes: Manaus–Santarém–Belém and Manaus–Tabatinga. Overcrowding can be a problem.

The cheapest way to travel is **hammock class**, out in the open on the deck. Be sure to take water, a cable and padlock for your bags, a jumper (nights on the water can be cool) a good book and, most importantly, a *rede* (hammock) with two pieces of rope (each about 1 m long) to string it up across the beams. The boats that travel on the Amazon itself are largely mosquito free – except when they moor; it's a good idea to bring a *mosquiteiro para rede* (mosquito net) for your hammock. Hammocks and nets can be bought easily in any of the larger Amazon towns, usually in the downtown area near the river. Arrive early to get a good spot. Some boats also have air-conditioned berths and **cabins** and, for a higher price, **suites** with attached bathroom.

Many boats ply the following routes: Manaus–Belém via Parintins, Óbidos and Santarém (four days); Manaus–São Gabriel da Cachoeira via Barcelos and Santa Isabel (six days); Manaus–Porto Velho via Manicoré and Humaitá (four days); Manaus–Tefé (36 hours); Manaus–Parintins (20 hours); Manaus–Tabatinga (six days); Belém–Santarém (two to three days); Belém–Macapá (36 hours); Macapá–Manaus (seven to 10 days).

Where to stay in the Brazilian Amazon

There is a good range of accommodation options in Brazil. An *albergue* or hostel offers the cheapest option. These have dormitory beds and single and double rooms. Many are part of the IYHA, www.iyha.org. **Hostel world**, www.hostelworld.com; **Hostel Bookers**, www.hostelbookers.com; and **Hostel.com**, www.hostel.com, are useful portals. **Hostel Trail Latin America** – T0131-208 0007 (UK), www.hosteltrail.com – managed from their hostel in Popayan, is an online network of hotels and tour companies in South America. A *pensão* is either a cheap guesthouse or a household that rents out some rooms.

A *pousada* is either a bed-and-breakfast, often small and family-run, or a sophisticated and often charming small hotel. A *hotel* is as it is anywhere else in the world, operating according to the international star system, although five-star hotels are not price controlled and hotels in any category are not always of the standard of their star equivalent in the USA, Canada or Europe. Many of the older hotels can be cheaper than hostels. Usually accommodation prices include a breakfast of rolls, ham, cheese, cakes and fruit with coffee and juice; there is no reduction if you don't eat it. Rooms vary too. Normally an *apartamento* is a room with separate living and sleeping areas and sometimes cooking facilities. A *quarto* is a standard room; *com banheiro* is en suite; and *sem banheiro* is with shared bathroom. Finally there are the *motels*. These should not be confused with their US counterpart: motels are used by guests not intending to sleep; there is no stigma attached and they usually offer good value (the rate for a full night is called the '*pernoite*'), however the decor can be a little garish.

It's a good idea to book accommodation in advance in small towns that are popular at weekends with city dwellers (eg near São Paulo and Rio de Janeiro), and it's essential to book at peak times.

Luxury accommodation

Much of the luxury private accommodation sector can be booked through operators. **Angatu**, www.angatu.com, offers the best private homes along the Costa Verde, together with bespoke trips. **Dehouche**, www.dehouche.com, offers upmarket accommodation and trips in Bahia, Rio and Alagoas. **Brazilian Beach House**, www.brazilianbeach house.com, has some of the finest houses in Búzios and Trancoso but is not so great at

Price codes

Where to stay

$$$$ over US$150

$$$ US$66-150

$$ US$30-65

$ Under US$30

Prices include taxes and service charge, but not meals. They are based on a double room, except in the **$** range, where prices are almost always per person.

Restaurants

$$$ Expensive over US$20

$$ Mid-range US$8-20

$ Cheap under US$8

Prices refer to the cost of a two-course meal, not including drinks.

organizing transfers and pick-ups. **Matuete**, www.matuete.com, has a range of luxurious properties and tours throughout Brazil.

Homestays

Staying with a local family is an excellent way to become integrated quickly into a city and companies try to match guests to their hosts. **Cama e Café**, www.camaecafe.com.br, organizes homestays in Rio de Janeiro, Olinda and a number of other cities around Brazil. **Couch surfing**, www.couchsurfing.com, offers a free, backpacker alternative.

Quality hotel associations

The better international hotel associations have members in Brazil. These include: **Small Luxury Hotels of the World**, www.slh.com; the **Leading Hotels of the World**, www.lhw.com; the **Leading Small Hotels of the World**, www.leadingsmallhotels oftheworld.com; **Great Small Hotels**, www.greatsmallhotels.com; and the **French Relais et Chateaux group**, www.relaischateaux.com, which also includes restaurants.

The Brazilian equivalent of these associations is the **Roteiros de Charme**, www.roteiros decharme.com.br, with some 30 locations in the southeast and northeast. Whilst membership of these groups pretty much guarantees quality, it is by no means comprehensive. There are many fine hotels and charming *pousadas* listed in our text that are not included in these associations.

Online travel agencies (OTAs)

Services like **Tripadvisor** and OTAs associated with them, such as **hotels.com, expedia.com** and **venere.com**, are well worth using for both reviews and for booking ahead. Hotels booked through an OTA can be up to 50% cheaper than the rack rate. Similar sites operate for hostels (though discounts are far less considerable). They include the **Hostelling International** site, www.hihostels.com, **hostelbookers.com, hostels.com** and **hostelworld.com**.

Food and drink in the Brazilian Amazon

Amazon food

The Amazon has a distinctive range of dishes that make use of the thousands of fruits and vegetables and the abundant fish of the area. Regional food here vies with Bahia as the best in Brazil – especially in Belém, Manaus and Rio Branco. Must-tries include *tacacá*, a soup made with jambo leaves, which numbs the tongue and stimulates energy. The best fish are *pacu* and *tambaqui*, both types of vegetarian piranha (the carnivorous ones can be eaten too). *Jaraqui* is very common in Amazonas – often in a delicious broth. *Pirarucu*, one of the world's largest freshwater fish, is delicious; however, due to overfishing it is in danger of becoming extinct and should only be eaten when sustainably sourced from locations such as Mamirauá. Specialities of Pará state include duck, often served as *pato no tucupi*, in a yellow soup made from the sieved off cassava (manioc) juice and served with *jambo*. *Maniçoba* is made with the poisonous leaves of the *cassava* (bitter manioc), simmered for eight days to get rid of the cyanide. It is jet black but deliciously tangy. *Caldeirada* is a fish and vegetable soup, served with *pirão* (manioc puree), and is a speciality of Amazonas. There is also an enormous variety of tropical and jungle fruits, many unique to the region. Try them fresh, or in ice creams or juices. The best include *tapereba*, *cupuaçu*, *cajú* (the fruit of the cashew nut), *cacau* (the fruit of the cocoa bean) and *camu camu*, which has the highest vitamin C content of any fruit in the world. Avoid food from street vendors, except those selling *tacacá* at the Boi bumba or from **Gisela** in the Praça São Sebastião in Manaus who has been selling delicious *tacacá* for decades, from 1600-2200.

Eating cheaply

The cheapest dish is the *prato feito* or *sortido*, an excellent-value set menu usually comprising meat/chicken/fish, beans, rice, chips and salad. The *prato comercial* is similar but rather better and a bit more expensive. Portions are usually large enough for two and come with two plates. If you are on your own, you could ask for an *embalagem* (doggy bag) or a *marmita* (takeaway) and offer it to a person with no food (many Brazilians do). Many restaurants serve *comida por kilo* buffets where you serve yourself and pay for the weight of food on your plate. This is generally good value and is a good option for vegetarians. *Lanchonetes* and *padarias* (diners and bakeries) are good for cheap eats; usually serving *prato feitos*, *salgadinhos*, excellent juices and other snacks.

The main meal is usually taken in the middle of the day; cheap restaurants tend not to be open in the evening.

Drink

The national liquor is *cachaça* (also known as *pinga*), which is made from sugar-cane, and ranging from cheap supermarket and service-station fire-water, to boutique distillery and connoisseur labels from the interior of Minas Gerais. Mixed with fruit juice, sugar and crushed ice, *cachaça* becomes the principal element in a *batida*, a refreshing but deceptively powerful drink. Served with pulped lime or other fruit, mountains of sugar and smashed ice it becomes the world's favourite party cocktail, caipirinha. A less potent caipirinha made with vodka is called a *caipiroska* and with sake a *saikirinha* or *caipisake*.

Some genuine Scotch whisky brands are bottled in Brazil. They are far cheaper even than duty free; Teacher's is the best. Locally made and cheap gin, vermouth and campari are pretty much as good as their US and European counterparts.

Wine is becoming increasingly popular, with good-value Portuguese and Argentinean bottles and some reasonable national table wines such as Château d'Argent, Château Duvalier, Almadén, Dreher, Preciosa and more respectable Bernard Taillan, Marjolet from Cabernet grapes, and the Moselle-type white Zahringer. A new *adega* tends to start off well, but the quality gradually deteriorates with time; many vintners have switched to American Concorde grapes, producing a rougher wine. Greville Brut champagne-style sparkling wine is inexpensive and very drinkable.

Brazil is the third most important wine producer in South America. The wine industry is mainly concentrated in the south of the country where the conditions are most suitable, with over 90% of wine produced in Rio Grande do Sul. There are also vineyards in Pernambuco. There are some interesting sparkling wines in the Italian spumante style (the best is Casa Valduga Brut Premium Sparkling Wine), and Brazil produces still wines using many international and imported varieties. None are distinguished – these are drinkable table wines at best. At worst they are plonk of the Blue Nun variety. The best bottle of red is probably the Boscato Reserva Cabernet Sauvignon. But it's expensive (at around US$20 a bottle); you'll get far higher quality and better value buying Portuguese, Argentine or Chilean wines in Brazil.

Brazilian beer is generally lager, served ice-cold. Draught beer is called *chope* or *chopp* (after the German Schoppen, and pronounced 'shoppi'). There are various national brands of bottled beers, which include Brahma, Skol, Cerpa, Antartica and the best Itaipava and Bohemia. There are black beers too, notably Xingu. They tend to be sweet. The best beer is from the German breweries in Rio Grande do Sul and is available only there.

Brazil's myriad fruits are used to make fruit juices or *sucos*, which come in a delicious variety, unrivalled anywhere in the world. *Açai, acerola, caju* (cashew), *pitanga, goiaba* (guava), *genipapo, graviola* (chirimoya), *maracujá* (passion fruit), *sapoti, umbu* and *tamarindo* are a few of the best. *Vitaminas* are thick fruit or vegetable drinks with milk. *Caldo de cana* is sugar-cane juice, sometimes mixed with ice. *Água de côco* or *côco verde* is coconut water served straight from a chilled, fresh, green coconut. The best known of many local soft drinks is *guaraná*, which is a very popular carbonated fruit drink, completely unrelated to the Amazon nut. The best variety is *guaraná Antarctica*. Coffee is ubiquitous and good tea entirely absent.

Festivals in the Brazilian Amazon

Brazil has festivals all year round with most concentrated in June and around Carnaval at the beginning of Lent. This list barely skims the surface.

February/March
Carnaval, Brazil's biggest festival takes place throughout the country and most famously in Rio's *sambódromo* stadium.

How big is your footprint?

→ Where possible choose a destination, tour operator or hotel with a proven ethical and environmental commitment – if in doubt, ask.

→ Spend money on locally produced (rather than imported) goods and services, buy directly from the producer or from a 'fair trade' shop, and use common sense when bargaining – the few dollars you save may be a week's salary to others.

→ Use water and electricity carefully – travellers may receive preferential supply while the needs of local communities are overlooked.

→ Learn about local etiquette and culture – consider local norms and behaviour and dress appropriately for local cultures and situations.

→ Protect wildlife and other natural resources – don't buy souvenirs or goods unless they are sustainably produced and are not protected under CITES legislation.

→ Always ask before taking photographs or videos of people.

→ Consider staying in local accommodation rather than foreign-owned hotels – the economic benefits for host communities are greater – and there are more opportunities to learn about local culture.

→ Within cities, local buses and (in São Paulo) metrôs are fast, cheap and have extensive routes. Try one instead of a taxi, and meet some real Brazilians!

→ Long-distance buses may take longer than flying but they have comfortable reclining seats, some offer drinks, and show up-to-date DVDs. They sometimes have better schedules too.

→ Supermarkets will give you a plastic bag for even the smallest purchases. If you don't need one, let them know – plastic waste is a huge problem – particularly in the northeast. When buying certain drinks, look for the returnable glass bottles.

→ Make a voluntary contribution to Climate Care, www.co2.org, to help counteract the pollution caused by tax-free fuel on your flight.

April
Festa do Açaí, **Festa da Castanha and Festa do Cupuaçu**, Codajás, Tefé and Presidente Figueiredo, Amazonas. 3 festivals devoted to 3 of the best Amazonian foods: the *açai* energy berry, *cupuaçu* and the Brazil nut.

June
Boi Bumba, Parintins, Amazonas. A huge spectacle re-enacting the Boi story, with large floats and troupes of dancers. On an island in the Amazon. See www.boibumba.com.
Bumba-Meu-Boi, São Luís, Maranhão, see www.saoluisturismo.com.br.
Festas Juninas (Festas do São João), Campina Grande, Paraíba, Caruaru, Pernambuco and throughout Brazil. Brazil's major winter festival when everyone dresses up as a yokel, drinks hot spiced wine and dances *forró*.

November
Círio de Nazaré, Belém and throughout Pará and Amazonas states. One of the largest religious celebrations in Brazil. Huge crowds, long processions and many live music and cultural events. See www.paratur.pa.gov.br.

Responsible travel

Sustainable or ecotourism is not just about looking after the physical environment, but also the local community. Whilst it has been slow to catch up with Costa Rica or Ecuador, Brazil now has some first-rate ecotourism projects and the country is a pioneer in urban community tourism in the favelas. Model ecotourism resorts in the forest include **Pousada Uacari** (page 91).

In the Amazon, Atlantic coast forest and parts of the *cerrado*, access to certain wilderness areas is restricted to scientists. Having such a low-impact policy over these regions means that their environment is protected from damage or over-use. In much of coastal Brazil, where tourism and property speculation has boomed in the last few years, the impact on local communities is particularly devastating. Some state governments cheerfully exploit the colourful local culture while sharing little of the profit. So rather than staying in a big resort and organizing a tour from back home, seek out smaller locally owned hotels and local indigenous guides. Try to visit projects such as the **Pataxó Reserve** in Jaqueira, Porto Seguro, and support the Caiçaras near Paraty.

Essentials A-Z

Accident and emergency
Ambulance T192. **Police** T190. If robbed or attacked, contact the tourist police. If you need to claim on insurance, make sure you get a police report.

Electricity
Generally 110 V 60 cycles AC, but in some cities and areas 220 V 60 cycles AC is used. European and U.S 2-pin plugs and sockets.

Embassies and consulates
For embassies and consulates of Brazil, see www.embassiesabroad.com.

Health → *Hospitals/medical services are listed in the Directory sections of each chapter.*
See your GP or travel clinic at least 6 weeks before departure for general advice on travel risks and vaccinations. Try phoning a specialist travel clinic if your own doctor is unfamiliar with health in the region. Make sure you have sufficient medical travel insurance, get a dental check, know your own blood group and, if you suffer a long-term condition such as diabetes or epilepsy, obtain a **Medic Alert** bracelet (www.medicalalert.co.uk).

There is a danger of **malaria** in Amazônia, especially on the brown-water rivers. Mosquito larvae do not breed well in the black-water rivers as they are too acidic. Mosquito nets are not required when in motion as boats travel away from the banks and are too fast for mosquitos to settle. However, nets and repellent can be useful for night stops. Wear long, loose trousers (tight ones are easy to bite through) and a baggy shirt at night and put repellent around shirt collars, cuffs and the tops of socks.

A **yellow fever** inoculation is strongly advised. It is compulsory to have a certificate when crossing borders and those without one will have to get inoculated and wait 10 days before travelling. Other common infections in the Amazon are **dengue**, which is widespread in the Amazon – as it is throughout South America – **cutaneous larva migrans** (a spot that appears to move), which is easily treated with **Thiabendazole**, and **tropical ulcers**, caught by scratching mosquito bites, which then get dirty and become infected. It is advisable to vaccinate against polio, tetanus, typhoid, hepatitis A and, for more remote areas, rabies. Cholera, diptheria and hepatitis B vaccinations are sometimes advised. Specialist advice should be taken on the best antimalarials to take before you leave.

Websites
www.cdc.gov Centres for Disease Control and Prevention (USA).
www.dh.gov.uk/en/Policyandguidance/ Healthadvicefortravellers/index.htm Department of Health advice for travellers.
www.fitfortravel.scot.nhs.uk Fit for Travel (UK), a site from Scotland providing a quick A-Z of vaccine and travel health advice requirements for each country.
www.fco.gov.uk Foreign and Commonwealth Office (FCO), UK.
www.itg.be Prince Leopold Institute for Tropical Medicine.
www.nathnac.org National Travel Health Network and Centre (NaTHNaC).
www.who.int World Health Organisation.

Books
Dawood, R, editor, *Travellers' health*, 3rd ed, Oxford: Oxford University Press, 2002.
Warrell, David, and Sarah Anderson, editors, *Expedition Medicine*, The Royal Geographic Society, ISBN 1 86197 040-4.
Wilson-Howarth, Jane. *Bugs, Bites and Bowels: the essential guide to travel health*, Cadogan 2006.

Internet

Brazil is said to be 7th in the world in terms of internet use. Public internet access is so readily available that it is almost pointless to list the locations. There is internet access on every other street corner in even the smallest towns and cities – look for signs saying '**LAN house**' or '**ciber-café**'. There is usually an hourly charge of around US$2, but you can almost always use partial hours at a reduced rate. More and more hotels offer an internet service to their guests – many in-room wireless; usually free but sometimes at exorbitant rates, while some government programmes even offer free use (notably in Manaus and Cuiaba) in public areas. For a regularly updated list of locations around the world, check www.netcafe guide.com.

Language → *See also page 120.*

Brazilians speak Portuguese, and very few speak anything else. Spanish may help you to be understood a little, but spoken Portuguese will remain undecipherable even to fluent Spanish speakers. Learn some Portuguese before arriving. Brazilians are the best thing about the country and without Portuguese you will not be able to interact beyond stereotypes and second guesses. Language classes are available in the larger cities. **Cactus** (www.cactuslanguage.com), **Languages abroad** (www.languagesabroad.co.uk) and **Travellers Worldwide** (www.travellersworld wide.com) are among the companies that can organize language courses in Brazil. **McGraw Hill** and **DK** (*Hugo Portuguese in Three Months*) offer the best teach-yourself books. **Sonia Portuguese** (www.sonia- portuguese.com) is a useful online resource.

Money

Currency

→ *£1 = R$3.03; US$1 = R$1.87 (May 2012).*
The unit of currency is the **real**, R$ (plural **reais**). Any amount of foreign currency and 'a

reasonable sum' in reais can be taken in, but sums over US$10,000 must be declared. Residents may only take out the equivalent of US$4000. Notes in circulation are: 100, 50, 10, 5 and 1 real; coins: 1 real, 50, 25, 10, 5 and 1 centavo. **Note** The exchange-rate fluctuates – check regularly.

Costs of travelling

Brazil is more expensive than other countries in South America. As a very rough guide, prices are about two-thirds those of Western Europe and a little cheaper than rural USA; though prices vary hugely according to the current exchange rate and strength of the real, whose value has soared since 2008 – with Goldman Sachs and Bloomberg considering the *real* to be the most over-valued major currency in the world in 2009-2010. It is expected to lose value; check on the latest before leaving on currency exchange sites such as www.x-rates.com.

Hostel beds are usually around US$15. Budget hotels with few frills have rooms for as little as US$30, and you should have no difficulty finding a double room costing US$45 wherever you are. Rooms are often pretty much the same price whether 1 or 2 people are staying. Eating is generally inexpensive, especially in *padarias* or *comida por kilo* (pay by weight) restaurants, which offer a wide range of food (salads, meat, pasta, vegetarian). Expect to pay around US$6 to eat your fill in a good-value restaurant. Although bus travel is cheap by US or European standards, because of the long distances, costs can soon mount up. Internal flights prices have come down dramatically in the last couple of years and some routes work out cheaper than taking a bus – especially if booking through the internet. Prices vary regionally. Ipanema is almost twice as expensive as rural Bahia. A can of beer in a supermarket in the southeast costs US$0.80, a litre of water US$0.60, a single metrô ticket in São Paulo US$1.60, a bus ticket between

US$1 and US$1.50 (depending on the city) and a cinema ticket around US$3.60.

ATMs

ATMs, or cash machines, are common in Brazil. As well as being the most convenient way of withdrawing money, they frequently offer the best available rates of exchange. They are usually closed after 2130 in large cities. There are 2 international ATM acceptance systems, **Plus** and **Cirrus**. Many issuers of debit and credit cards are linked to one, or both (eg Visa is Plus, MasterCard is Cirrus). **Bradesco** and **HSBC** are the 2 main banks offering this service. **Red Banco 24 Horas** kiosks advertise that they take a long list of credit cards in their ATMs, including MasterCard and Amex, but international cards cannot always be used; the same is true of **Banco do Brasil**.

There are plenty of ATM facilities in all the Amazon's main towns (the state capitals, Santarém, Cruzeiro do Sul, Marabá, Parintins and São Gabriel da Cachoeira), where there is an **HSBC**, **Bradesco** or **Banco 24 horas**. Small amounts of US dollars cash can usually be exchanged away from banks at a poor rate, but are not accepted as local currency. The rate of exchange for traveller's cheques is appalling.

Advise your bank before leaving, as cards are usually stopped in Brazil without prior warning. Find out before you leave what international functionality your card has. Check if your bank or credit card company imposes handling charges. Internet banking is useful for monitoring your account or transferring funds. Do not rely on 1 card, in case of loss. If you do lose a card, immediately contact the 24-hr helpline of the issuer in your home country (keep this number in a safe place).

Exchange

Banks in major cities will change cash and traveller's cheques (Tcs), but the rate of exchange for traveller's cheques is appalling. . If you keep the official exchange slips, you may convert back into foreign currency up to 50% of the amount you exchanged. The parallel market, found in travel agencies, exchange houses and among hotel staff, often offers marginally better rates than the banks but commissions can be very high. Many banks may only change US$300 minimum in cash, US$500 in TCs. Rates for TCs are usually far lower than for cash, they are harder to change and a very heavy commission may be charged. Dollars cash (take US$5 or US$10 bills) are not useful as alternative currency. Brazilians use *reais*.

Credit cards

Credit cards are widely used, athough often they are not usable in the most unlikely of places, such as tour operators. **Diners Club**, **MasterCard**, **Visa** and **Amex** are useful. Cash advances on credit cards will only be paid in *reais* at the tourist rate, incurring at least a 1.5% commission. Banks in small, remote places may still refuse to give a cash advance: try asking for the *gerente* (manager).

Money transfers

Money sent to Brazil is normally paid out in Brazilian currency, so do not have more money sent out than you need for your stay. Funds can ostensibly be received within 48 banking hours, but it can take at least a month to arrive, allowing banks to capitalize on your transfer. The documentation required to receive it varies according to the whim of the bank staff, making the whole procedure often far more trouble than it is worth. ·

Opening hours

Generally Mon-Fri 0900-1800; closed for lunch some time between 1130 and 1400. **Shops** Also open on Sat until 1230 or 1300. **Government offices** Mon-Fri 1100-1800. **Banks** Mon-Fri 1000-1600 or 1630; closed at weekends.

Safety

Although Brazil's big cities suffer high rates of violent crime, this is mostly confined to the favelas (slums) where poverty and drugs are the main cause. Visitors should not enter favelas except when accompanied by workers for NGOs, tour groups or other people who know the local residents well and are accepted by the community. Otherwise they may be targets of muggings by armed gangs who show short shrift to those who resist them. Mugging can take place anywhere. Travel light after dark with few valuables (avoid wearing jewellery and use a cheap, plastic, digital watch). Ask hotel staff where is and isn't safe; crime is patchy in Brazilian cities.

If the worst does happen and you are threatened, don't panic, and hand over your valuables. Do not resist, and report the crime to the local tourist police later. It is extremely rare for a tourist to be hurt during a robbery in Brazil. Being aware of the dangers, acting confidently and using your common sense will reduce many of the risks.

Photocopy your passport, air ticket and other documents, make a record of traveller's cheque and credit card numbers. Keep them separately from the originals and leave another set of records at home. Keep all documents secure; hide your main cash supply in different places or under your clothes. Extra pockets sewn inside shirts and trousers, money belts (best worn below the waist), neck or leg pouches and elasticated support bandages for keeping money above the elbow or below the knee have been repeatedly recommended.

All border areas should be regarded with some caution because of smuggling activities. Violence over land ownership in parts of the interior have resulted in a 'Wild West' atmosphere in some towns, which should therefore be passed through quickly. Red-light districts should also be given a wide berth as there are reports of drinks being drugged with a substance popularly known as 'good night Cinderella'. This leaves the victim easily amenable to having their possesions stolen, or worse.

Avoiding cons

Never trust anyone telling sob stories or offering 'safe rooms', and when looking for a hotel, always choose the room yourself. Be wary of 'plain-clothes policemen'; insist on seeing identification and on going to the police station by main roads. Do not hand over your identification (or money) until you are at the station. On no account take them directly back to your hotel. Be even more suspicious if they seek confirmation of their status from a passer-by.

Hotel security

Hotel safe deposits are generally, but not always, secure. If you cannot get a receipt for valuables in a hotel safe, you can seal the contents in a plastic bag and sign across the seal. Always keep an inventory of what you have deposited. If you don't trust the hotel, lock everything in your pack and secure it in your room when you go out. If you lose valuables, report to the police and note details of the report for insurance purposes. Be sure to be present whenever your credit card is used.

Police

There are several types of police: **Polícia Federal**, civilian dressed, who handle all federal law duties, including immigration. A subdivision is the **Polícia Federal Rodoviária**, uniformed, who are the traffic police on federal highways. **Polícia Militar** are the uniformed, street police force, under the control of the state governor, handling all state laws. They are not the same as the Armed Forces' internal police. **Polícia Civil**, also state controlled, handle local laws and investigations. They are usually in civilian dress, unless in the traffic division. In cities, the **Prefeitura** controls the **Guarda**

Municipal, who handle security. **Tourist police** operate in places with a strong tourist presence. In case of difficulty, visitors should seek out tourist police in the first instance.

Public transport

When you have all your luggage with you at a bus or railway station, be especially careful and carry any shoulder bags in front of you. To be extra safe, take a taxi between the airport/bus station/railway station and hotel, keep your bags with you and pay only when you and your luggage are outside; avoid night buses and arriving at your destination at night.

Women travellers

Most of these tips apply to any single traveller. When you set out, err on the side of caution until your instincts have adjusted to the customs of a new culture.

Be prepared for the exceptional curiosity extended to visitors, especially women, and try not to overreact. If, as a single woman, you can befriend a local woman, you will learn much more about the country you are visiting. There is a definite 'gringo trail' you can follow, which can be helpful when looking for safe accommodation, especially if arriving after dark (best avoided). Remember that for a single woman a taxi at night can be as dangerous as walking alone. It is easier for men to take the friendliness of locals at face value; women may be subject to unwanted attention. Do not disclose to strangers where you are staying.

By wearing a wedding ring and saying that your 'husband' is close at hand, you may dissuade an aspiring suitor. If politeness fails, do not feel bad about showing offence and departing. A good rule is always to act with confidence, as though you know where you are going, even if you do not. Someone who looks lost is more likely to attract unwanted attention.

Tax

Airport departure tax The amount of tax depends on the class and size of the airport, but the cost is usually incorporated into the ticket.

VAT Rates vary from 7-25% at state and federal level; the average is 17-20%.

Telephone

→ *Country code: +55.*
Ringing: equal tones with long pauses.
Engaged: equal tones, equal pauses.

Making a phone call in Brazil can be confusing. It is necessary to dial a 2-digit telephone company code prior to the area code for all calls. Phone numbers are now printed in this way: 0XX21 (0 for a national call, XX for the code of the phone company chosen (eg 31 for Telemar) followed by, 21 for Rio de Janeiro, for example and the 8-digit number of the subscriber. The same is true for international calls where 00 is followed by the operator code and then the country code and number.

Telephone operators and their codes are: **Embratel**, 21 (nationwide); **Telefônica**, 15 (state of São Paulo); **Telemar**, 31 (Alagoas, Amazonas, Amapá, Bahia, Ceará, Espírito Santo, Maranhão, most of Minas Gerais, Pará, Paraíba, Pernambuco, Piauí, Rio de Janeiro, Rio Grande do Norte, Roraima, Sergipe); **Tele Centro-Sul**, 14 (Acre, Goiás, Mato Grosso, Mato Grosso do Sul, Paraná, Rondônia, Santa Catarina, Tocantins and the cities of Brasília and Pelotas); **CTBC-Telecom**, 12 (some parts of Minas Gerais, Goiás, Mato Grosso do Sul and São Paulo state); **Intelig**, 23.

National calls

Telephone booths or *orelhões* (literally 'big ears' as they are usually ear-shaped, fibreglass shells) are easy to come by in towns and cities. Local phone calls and telegrams are cheap.

Cartões telefônicos (phone cards) are available from newsstands, post offices and some chemists. They cost US$4 for 30 units and up to US$7 for 90 units. Local calls from a private phone are often free. *Cartões telefônicos internacionais* (international phone cards) are increasingly available in tourist areas and are often sold at hostels.

Mobile phones

Cellular phones are widespread and coverage excellent even in remote areas, but prices are extraordinarily high and users still pay to receive calls outside the metropolitan area where their phone is registered. SIM cards are hard to buy as users require a CPF (a Brazilian social security number) to buy one, but phones can be hired. When using a cellular telephone you do not drop the zero from the area code as you have when dialling from a fixed line.

Time

Brazil has 4 time zones: Brazilian standard time is GMT-3; the Amazon time zone (Pará west of the Rio Xingu, Amazonas, Roraima, Rondônia, Mato Grosso and Mato Grosso do Sul) is GMT-4, the State of Acre is GMT-5; and the Fernando de Noronha archipelago is GMT-2. Clocks move forward 1 hr in summer for approximately 5 months (usually between Oct and Feb or Mar), but times of change vary. This does not apply to Acre.

Tipping

Tipping is not usual, but always appreciated as staff are often paid a pittance. In restaurants, add 10% of the bill if no service charge is included; cloakroom attendants deserve a small tip; porters have fixed charges but often receive tips as well; unofficial car parkers on city streets should be tipped 2 reais.

Tour operators

UK

Austral Tours, 20 Upper Tachbrook St, London SW1V 1SH, T020-7233 5384,
www.latinamerica.co.uk. Tours to Rio, the Amazon and the northeast.

Condor Journeys and Adventures, 2 Ferry Bank, Colintraive, Argyll PA22 3AR, T01700-841 318, www.condorjourneys-adventures.com. Tailor-made journeys to standard destinations.

Explore Worldwide, 1 Frederick St, Aldershot, Hants GU11 1LQ, T01252-760 000, www.exploreworldwide.com. Standard small-group trips to the northeast, Amazon and Rio.

Journey Latin America, 12-13 Heathfield Terr, Chiswick, London W4 4JE, T020-8747 8315, www.journeylatinamerica.co.uk. Long-established company with excellent escorted tours to some interesting areas like Goiás and the Chapada Diamantina. They also offer a wide range of good-value flight options.

Last Frontiers, The Mill, Quainton Rd, Waddesdon, Bucks HP18 0LP, T01296-653000, www.lastfrontiers.com. Imaginative tailor-made tours to some interesting out-of-the-way locations including Fernando de Noronha.

Select Latin America, 3.51 Canterbury Court, 1-3 Brixton Rd, Kennington Park Business Centre, London SW9 6DE, T020-7407 1478, www.selectlatinamerica.co.uk. Quality tailor-made holidays and small group tours.

Naturetrek, Cheriton Mill, Cheriton, Alresford, Hants SO24 0NG, T01962-733051; www.nature trek.co.uk. Wildlife tours throughout Brazil with bespoke options and specialist birding tours of the Atlantic coastal rainforests.

Reef and Rainforest Tours Ltd, A7 Dart Marine Park, Steamer Quay, Totnes, Devon, TQ9 5DR, T01803-866965, www.reefandrainforest.co.uk. Specialists in tailor-made and group wildlife tours.

Songlines Music Travel, T020-8505 2582, www.songlines.co.uk/musictravel . Specialist Carnaval packages in Bahia and São Paulo with a break on the beach afterwards. Tour guides offer the chance to meet many of the musicians and to hear the best live music as well as attend the key Carnaval shows.

Steppes Latin America, 51 Castle St, Cirencester, Glos GL7 1QD, T01285-885333, www.steppestravel.co.uk. Tailor-made and group itineraries throughout Brazil and Latin America.

Sunvil Latin America, Sunvil House, Upper Square, Old Isleworth, Middlesex TW7 7BJ, T020-8568 4499, www.sunvil.co.uk. A good range of options throughout Brazil, including some out-of-the-way destinations.

Tell Tale Travel, 25a Kensington Church St, 1st floor, London T0800-011 2571; www.telltaletravel.co.uk. Imaginative and well-researched bespoke holidays throughout Brazil, with homestays and light adventure trips aiming to integrate locals and visitors and show Brazil from a Brazilian perspective.

Trips Worldwide, 14 Frederick Place, Clifton, Bristol BS8 1AS, T0117-311 4400, www.tripsworldwide.co.uk. Tailor-made trips throughout South America.

Veloso Tours, ground floor, 34 Warple Way, London W3 0RG, T020-8762 0616, www.veloso.com. An imaginative range of tours throughout Brazil and bespoke options on request.

Wildlife World Wide, Long Barn South, Sutton Manor Farm, Bishop's Sutton, Alresford, Hants SO24 0AA, www.wildlife worldwide.com. Wildlife trips to the Amazon (on board the Amazon Clipper), Pantanal, safaris on the Transpantaneira and Iguaçu; with bespoke options available.

Wildwings, 577-579 Fishponds Rd, Fishponds, Bristol BS16 3AF, T0117-965 8333, www.wildwings.co.uk. Jaguar tours around Porto Jofre in the Pantanal with extensions to the Atlantic coastal rainforests and elsewhere.

North America

4starSouth America, T1-800-887 5686, www.4starSouthAmerica.com. Customized or scheduled tours throughout South America.

Also has an office in Brazil at Av NS Copacabana 1066/907, Rio de Janeiro, T021-2267 6624.

Brazil For Less, 7201 Wood Hollow Dr, Austin, TX 78731, T1-877-565 8119 (US toll free) or T+44-203-006 2507 (UK), www.brazilforless.com. US-based travel firm with a focus solely on South America, with local offices and operations, and a price guarantee. Good-value tours, run by travellers for travellers. Will meet or beat any published rates on the internet from outside Brazil.

Ela Brasil Tours, 14 Burlington Dr, Norwalk, CT 06851, T203-840 9010, www.elabrasil.com. Excellent bespoke tours throughout Brazil to some very imaginative destinations. Uses only the best and most responsible local operators.

Ladatco Tours, 3006 Aviation Av 4C, Coconut Grove, Florida 33133, USA, T1800-327 6162, www.ladatco.com. Standard tours to Rio, Iguaçu and Manaus for the Amazon.

Mila Tours, 100 S Greenleaf Av, Gurnee, IL 60031-337, T847-248 2111, T800-387 7378 (USA and Canada), www.milatours.com. Itineraries to Rio, Iguaçu and the northeast.

Tropical Nature Travel, PO Box 5276, Gainesville, Fl 326270 5276, USA, T352-376 3377, www.tropicalnaturetravel.com. Ecotourism tours to *fazendas* in the northern and southern Pantanal, the Amazon (with Amazon Clipper), Iguaçu and the Mata Atlântica.

Brazil

Ambiental, Av Brigadeiro Faria Lima 156, Pinheiros, São Paulo, T011-3818 4600, www.ambiental.tur.br. Trips to every corner of Brazil from Jalapão and Fernando de Noronha to the Pantanal and Iguaçu.

Andy and Nadime Whittaker's Birding Brazil Tours, www.birdingbraziltours.com. Another good company, based in Manaus. The couple worked with the BBC Natural History Unit on David Attenborough's *The Life of Birds* and are ground agents for a number of the major birding tour companies from the US and Europe.

Brazil Always Summer, SEPS EQ 714/914, Bloco E, Sala 409, Edificio Talento, Brasilia-DF, CEP 70390-145, T061-3039 4442, www.brazilalwayssummer.com. Tour operator specializing in holidays to Brazil. Services include hotel booking, Rio Carnaval tickets and excellent car rental rates. English-speaking staff.

Brazil Nature Tours, R Guia Lopes 150, 1st floor, Campo Grande, MS, T067-3042 4659, www.brazilnaturetours.com. Booking agents for nature-based tours to the Pantanal and the Amazon.

Cariri Ecotours, R Francisco Gurgel, 9067, Ponta Negra Beach, Natal, T084-9928 0198, www.caririecotours.com.br. If ecotourism means wildlife then Manary are not eco at all, but they do offer unusual, exciting tours to the northeastern *sertão,* including the spectacular Serra da Capivara (to see the rock paintings), Cariri and the fossilized dinosaur prints in Paraíba. Very professional service.

Dehouche, T021-2512 3895, www.dehouche.com. Upmarket, carefully tailored trips throughout Brazil.

Matueté, T011-3071 4515, www.matuete.com. Bespoke luxury options around Brazil including a range of private house rentals.

Tatur Turismo, Av Tancredo Neves 274, Centro Empresarial Iguatemi, Sala 228, Bloco B, Salvador, 41820-020, Bahia, T071-3114 7900, www.tatur.com.br. Very helpful and professional bespoke Bahia-based agency who can organize tours throughout Brazil, especially in Bahia, using many of the smaller hotels.

whl.travel, T031-3889 8596, www.whlbrazil.com. Online network of tour operators for booking accommodation and tours throughout Brazil.

Tourist information

The **Ministério do Turismo**, Esplanada dos Ministérios, Bloco U, 2nd and 3rd floors, Brasilia, www.turismo.gov.br or www.braziltour.com, is in charge of tourism in Brazil and has information in many languages. **Embratur**, the Brazilian Institute of Tourism, is at the same address, and is in charge of promoting tourism abroad. For information and phone numbers for your country visit www.braziltour.com. Local tourist information bureaux are not usually helpful for information on cheap hotels – they generally just dish out pamphlets. Expensive hotels provide tourist magazines for their guests. Telephone directories (not Rio) contain good street maps.

Visas and immigration

Visas are not required for stays of up to 90 days by tourists from Andorra, Argentina, Austria, Bahamas, Barbados, Belgium, Bolivia, Chile, Colombia, Costa Rica, Denmark, Ecuador, Finland, France, Germany, Greece, Iceland, Ireland, Italy, Liechtenstein, Luxembourg, Malaysia, Monaco, Morocco, Namibia, the Netherlands, Norway, Paraguay, Peru, Philippines, Portugal, San Marino, South Africa, Spain, Suriname, Sweden, Switzerland, Thailand, Trinidad and Tobago, United Kingdom, Uruguay, the Vatican and Venezuela. For them, only the following documents are required at the port of disembarkation: a passport valid for at least 6 months (or *cédula de identidad* for nationals of Argentina, Chile, Paraguay and Uruguay); and a return or onward ticket, or adequate proof that you can purchase your return fare, subject to no remuneration being received in Brazil and no legally binding or contractual documents being signed. Venezuelan passport holders can stay for 60 days on filling in a form at the border.

Citizens of the USA, Canada, Australia, New Zealand and other countries not mentioned above, and anyone wanting to stay longer than 180 days, *must* get a visa before arrival, which may, if you ask, be granted for multiple entry. US citizens must be fingerprinted on entry to Brazil. Visa fees vary from country to country, so apply to the Brazilian consulate in your home country. The consular fee in the USA is US$55. Students planning to study in Brazil or employees of foreign companies can apply for a 1- or 2-year visa. 2 copies of the application form, 2 photos, a letter from the sponsoring company or educational institution in Brazil, a police form showing no criminal convictions and a fee of around US$80 is required.

Identification

You must always carry identification when in Brazil. Take a photocopy of the personal details in your passport, plus your Brazilian immigration stamp, and leave your passport in the hotel safe deposit. This photocopy, when authorized in a *cartório*, US$1, is a legitimate copy of your documents. Be prepared, however, to present the originals when travelling in sensitive border areas. Always keep an independent record of your passport details. Also register with your consulate to expedite document replacement if yours gets lost or stolen.

Warning Do not lose the entry/exit permit they give you when you enter Brazil. Leaving the country without it, you may have to pay up to US$100 per person. It is suggested that you photocopy this form and have it authenticated at a *cartório*, US$1, in case of loss or theft.

Weights and measures

Metric.

Contents

São Paulo

São Paulo

The city of São Paulo is vast and can feel intimidating at first. But this is a city of separate neighbourhoods, only a few of which are interesting for visitors and, once you have your base, it is easy to negotiate. Those who don't flinch from the city's size and who are prepared to spend money and time here, and who get to know Paulistanos, are seldom disappointed. (The inhabitants of the city are called Paulistanos, to differentiate them from the inhabitants of the state, who are called Paulistas.) Nowhere in Brazil is better for concerts, clubs, theatre, ballet, classical music, all round nightlife, restaurants and beautifully designed hotels.

Arriving in São Paolo → *Phone code: 011.*

Getting there There are air services from all parts of Brazil, Europe, North and South America to the international **airport** at Guarulhos, also known as Cumbica, Avenida Monteiro Lobato 1985, T2445 2945 (30 km northeast of the city). The local airport of Congonhas, 14 km south of the city centre on Avenida Washington Luiz, is used for the Rio-São Paulo shuttle. It receives some flights to Belo Horizonte and Vitória and private flights only, T5090 9000. The **main rodoviária** is Tietê (T2223 7152), which is very convenient and has its own Metrô station. There are three other bus stations for inter-state bus services. ▸▸ *See also Transport, page 37.*

Getting around and orientation Much of the centre is pedestrianized, so walking is the only option if you wish to explore it. The best and cheapest way to get around São Paulo is on the Metrô system, which is clean, safe, cheap and efficient, and being expanded. Bus routes can be confusing and slow due to frequent traffic jams, but buses are safe, clean and only crowded at peak hours. All the rodoviárias (bus stations) are on the Metrô, but if travelling with luggage, take a taxi. The **Old Centre** (Praça da República, Sé, Santa Cecília) is a place to visit but not to stay. The central commercial district, containing banks, offices and shops, is known as the Triângulo, bounded by Ruas Direita, 15 (Quinze) de Novembro, São Bento and Praça Antônio Prado, but it is rapidly spreading towards the Praça da República. **Jardins**, the city's most affluent inner neighbourhood, is a good place to stay and to visit, especially if you want to shop and eat well. Elegant little streets hide hundreds of wonderful restaurants and accommodation ranges from the luxurious to the top end of the budget range. You are safe here at night. The northeastern section of Jardins, known as **Cerqueira César**, abuts one of São Paulo's grandest modern avenues, **Paulista**, lined with skyscrapers, shops and a few churches and museums including MASP (Museu de Arte de São Paulo). There are metro connections from here and a number of good hotels. **Ibirapuera Park and around**: the inner city's largest green space is home to a handful of museums, running tracks, a lake and frequent free live concerts on Sun. The adjoining neighbourhoods of Moema and Vila Mariana have a few hotels, but **Moema, Itaim** and **Vila Olimpia** are among the nightlife centres of São Paulo with a wealth of streetside bars, designer restaurants and European-style dance clubs. Hotels tend to be expensive as they are near the new business centre on Avenidas Brigadeiro Faria Lima and Luis Carlos Berrini. **Pinheiros and Vila Madalena** are less chic, but equally lively at night and with the funkiest shops.

Beware of assaults and pickpocketing in São Paulo. Thieves often use the mustard-on-the-back trick to distract you while someone else robs you. The areas around Luz station, Praça da República and Centro are not safe at night, and do not enter favelas.

Tourist offices There are tourist information booths with English speaking staff in arrivals of terminals 1 and 2 at Guarulhos airport (Cumbica, 0600-2200); and tourist booths in the Tietê bus station (0600-2200) and in the following locations throughout the city: **Olido** ① *Av São João 473, Mon-Fri 0900-1800*; at Parque Prefeito Mário Covas ① *Av Paulista 1853, daily 0800-2000*; at the Mercado Municipal ① *R da Cantareira 306, Mon-Sat 0900-1800, Sun 0700-1600.* An excellent map is available free at all these offices, as well as free maps and pamphlets in English. Visit www.cidadedesaopaulo.com (Portuguese, English and Spanish), also www.guiasp.com.br for what's on and where to go. Editora Abril also publish maps and an excellent guide, *Guia de São Paolo - Sampa* (Portuguese), see www.abril.com.br.

Climate São Paulo sits on a plateau at around 800 m and the weather is temperamental. Rainfall is ample and temperatures fluctuate greatly: summer averages 20-30°C (occasionally peaking into the high 30s or 40s), winter temperatures are 15-25°C (occasionally dropping to below 10° C). The winter months (April-October) are also the driest, with minimal precipitation in June/July. Christmas and New Year are wet. When there are thermal inversions, air pollution can be troublesome.

Centro Histórico

A focal point of the centre is the **Parque Anhangabaú**, an open space between the Triângulo and the streets which lead to Praça da República (Metrô Anhangabaú is at its southern end). Beneath Anhangabaú, north-south traffic is carried by a tunnel. Crossing it are two viaducts: **Viaduto do Chá**, which is open to traffic and links Rua Direita and Rua Barão de Itapetininga. Along its length sellers of potions, cures, fortunes and trinkets set up their booths. The **Viaduto Santa Ifigênia**, an iron bridge for pedestrians only, connects Largo de São Bento with Largo de Santa Ifigênia.

On **Largo de São Bento** there is the **Igreja e Mosteiro de São Bento** ① *T3328 8799, www.mosteiro.org.br for details of all services, including Gregorian chant*, an early 20th-century building (1910-22) on the site of a 1598 chapel. Due south of São Bento is the **Martinelli building** ① *on R Líbero Badaró at Av São João, closed*, the city's first skyscraper (1922). It was surpassed by the **Edifício Banespa** (finished 1947) ① *R João Brícola 24, T3249 7180, Mon-Fri 1000-1700, US$4*, with 360° views from the top, up to 40 km, smog permitting. The renovated **Pateo do Collégio (Museu de Anchieta)** ① *Praça Pátio do Colégio, T3105 6899, www.pateodocollegio. com.br, Metrô Sé, with a café, Tue-Sun 0900-*

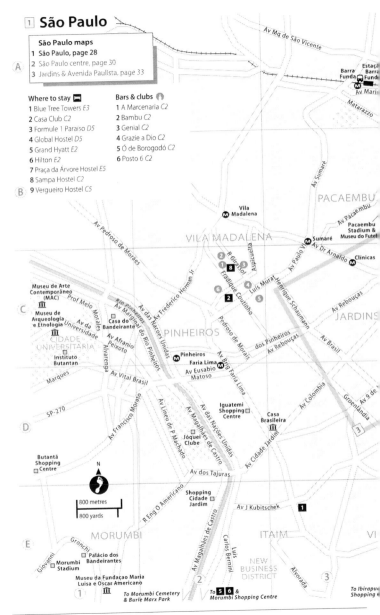

1 São Paulo

São Paulo maps
1 São Paulo, page 28
2 São Paulo centre, page 30
3 Jardins & Avenida Paulista, page 33

Where to stay 🛏
1 Blue Tree Towers *E3*
2 Casa Club *C2*
3 Formule 1 Paraiso *D5*
4 Global Hostel *D5*
5 Grand Hyatt *E2*
6 Hilton *E2*
7 Praça da Árvore Hostel *E5*
8 Sampa Hostel *C2*
9 Vergueiro Hostel *C5*

Bars & clubs 🍸
1 A Marcenaria *C2*
2 Bambu *C2*
3 Genial *C2*
4 Grazie a Dio *C2*
5 Ó de Borogodó *C2*
6 Posto 6 *C2*

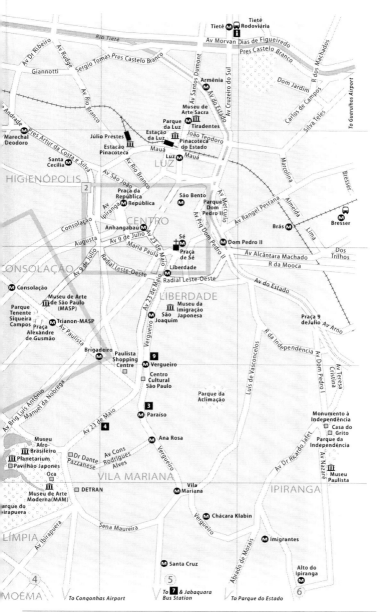

1700, US$3. It is an exact replica of the original Jesuit church and college but dates from 1950s. Most of the buildings are occupied by the Museu de Anchieta, named after the Jesuit captain who led the first mission. This houses, amongst other items a 17th-century font that was used to baptize *indígenas* and a collection of Guaraní art and artefacts from the colonial era and a modernist painting of the priest, by Italian Albino Menghini.

A short distance southeast of the Pateo do Collégio is the **Solar da Marquesa de Santos**, an 18th-century residential building, which now contains the **Museu da Cidade** ① *R Roberto Simonsen 136, T3241 1081, www.museudacidade.sp.gov.br, Tue-Sun 0900-1700*. The **Praça da Sé** is a huge open area south of the Pateo do Collégio, dominated by the **Catedral Metropolitana** ① *T3107 6832, Mon-Sat 0800-1700, Sun 0800-1830*, a massive, peaceful

2 São Paulo centre

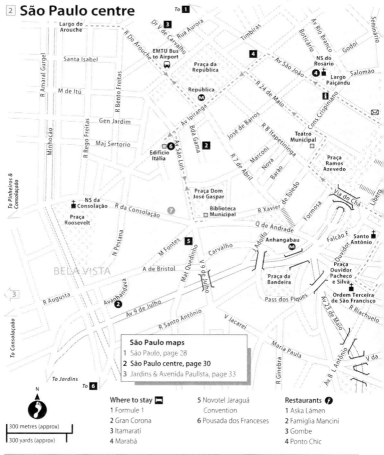

300 metres (approx)

300 yards (approx)

Where to stay 🛏
1 Formule 1
2 Gran Corona
3 Itamaratí
4 Marabá
5 Novotel Jaraguá Convention
6 Pousada dos Franceses

Restaurants 🍴
1 Aska Lámen
2 Famiglia Mancini
3 Gombe
4 Ponto Chic

space. The cathedral's foundations were laid more than 40 years before its inauguration during the 1954 festivities commemorating the fourth centenary of the city. It was fully completed in 1970. This enormous building in neo-Gothic style has a capacity for 8000 worshippers in its five naves. The interior is mostly unadorned, except for the two gilt mosaic pictures in the transepts: on the north side is the Virgin Mary and on the south Saint Paul.

West of the Praça da Sé, along Rua Benjamin Constant, is the Largo de São Francisco. Here is the **Igreja da Ordem Terceira de São Francisco** ① *T3105 6899, 0730-2000*. The convent was inaugurated in 1647 and reformed in 1744. To the right is the Igreja das Chagas do Seráphico Pai São Francisco (1787), painted like its neighbour in blue and gold. Across the Viaduto do Chá is the **Teatro Municipal** ① *T3223 3022*, one of the few distinguished early 20th- century survivors that São Paulo can boast. Viewing the interior may only be possible during a performance; as well as the full evening performances, look out for its midday, string quartet and 'vesperais líricas' concerts.

Praça da República

In Praça da República the trees are tall and shady. There are also lots of police. Near the Praça is the city's tallest building, the **Edifício Itália** ① *Av Ipiranga 344, T2189 2929, US$8*. There is a restaurant on top and a sightseeing balcony. If you walk up Avenida São Luís, which has many airline offices and travel agencies (especially found in the Galeria Metrópole), you arrive at Praça Dom José Gaspar, in which is the **Biblioteca Municipal Mário de Andrade**, surrounded by a pleasant shady garden.

North of the centre

About 10 minutes' walk from the centre is the old **Mercado Municipal** ① *R Cantareira 306, www.mercadomunicipal.com.br, Mon-Sat 0600-1800, Sun 0700-1600*, covering 27,000 sq m. **Parque da Luz** on Avenida Tiradentes (110,000 sq m) was formerly a botanical garden. It is next to the Luz railway station. There are two museums: in the park is the **Pinacoteca do Estado** (State Art Collection) ① *Praça da Luz 2, T3224 1000, www.pinacoteca.org.br, Tue-Sun 1000- 1800, US$3, free on Sat (closes 1730)*. It and its

5 Sushi Yassu
6 Terraço Italia

Bars & clubs 🎵
7 Royal Club

Historic buildings walk - ◀ - -

neighbouring sister gallery, the **Estação Pinacoteca** ① *Largo General Osório 66, T3337 0185, daily 1000-1730, US$2, Sat free*, preserve the best collection of modernist Brazilian art outside the Belas Artes in Rio, together with important works by Europeans like Picasso and Chagall. Both have good cafés, the Pinacoteca has a very good art bookshop. Nearby, the **Museu de Arte Sacra** ① *Av Tiradentes 676, T3326 1373, www.museu artesacra.org.br, Tue-Sun 1100-1900, US$2.25*, is modern and tasteful, housed in the serene **Igreja e Convento Nossa Senhora da Luz** (1774), still partially occupied. It has a priceless, beautifully presented collection including works by Aleijadinho, Benedito Calixto, Mestre Athayde and Francisco Xavier de Brito. The convent is one of the few colonial buildings left in São Paulo; the chapel dates from 1579.

Liberdade

Directly south of the Praça da Sé, and one stop on the Metrô, is Liberdade, the central Japanese district, now also home to large numbers of Koreans and Chinese. The Metrô station is in Praça da Liberdade, in which there is an oriental market every Sunday (see Shopping). The Praça is one of the best places in the city for Japanese food. **Museu da Imigração Japonesa** ① *R São Joaquim 381, exhibition on 7th, 8th and 9th floors, T3209 5465, www.nihonsite.com.br/muse, Tue-Sun 1330-1730, US$2.50*, is excellent, with a roof garden; captions have English summaries.

West of the Old Centre

Jardins and Avenida Paulista → *See map opposite.*

Avenida Paulista has been transformed since the 1890s from the city's most fashionable promenade into six lanes of traffic lined with banks' and multinationals' headquarters. Its highlight is undoubtedly **MASP**, the common name for the **Museu de Arte de São Paulo** ① *Av Paulista 1578 (above the 9 de Julho tunnel); T3251 5644, www.masp.art.br, Metrô Trianon-MASP; open 1100-1800, except Thu 1100-2000, closed Mon, US$8.20, Tue free*. The museum has the finest collection of European masters in the southern hemisphere with works by artists like Raphael, Bellini, Bosch, Rembrandt, Turner, Constable, Monet, Manet and Renoir. Also some interesting work by Brazilian artists, including Portinari. Temporary exhibitions are also held and when a popular show is on, it can take up to an hour to get in. There is a very good art shop.

Opposite MASP is **Parque Tenente Siqueira Campos** ① *daily 0700-1830*, which covers two blocks on either side of Alameda Santos; a bridge links the two parts of the park. It is block of subtropical forest in the busiest part of the city. In the foyers of some of the nearby towers are various cultural centres (eg **FIESP**, Av Paulista 1313) which put on worthwhile exhibitions and are more-or-less the only sights in the city open on a Monday. The **Museu da Imagem e do Som (MIS)** ① *Av Europa 158, T3085 1498, www.mis.sp.gov.br, Tue-Sun 1000-1800*, has photographic exhibitions, archives of Brazilian cinema and music, and a nice café. Next to MIS is the **Museu Brasiliero da Escultura** (MuBE); free to temporary exhibitions and recitals in the afternoons. Avenida Europa continues to Avenida Brigadeiro Faria Lima, on which is the **Casa Brasileira** ① *Av Faria Lima 2705, T3032 3727, www.mcb.sp.gov.br, Tue-Sun 1000-1800, US$2.20*, a museum of Brazilian furniture. It also holds temporary exhibitions.

Cidade Universitária and Morumbi

The Cidade Universitária is on the west bank of the Rio Pinheiros, opposite Pinheiros district. The campus also contains the famous **Instituto Butantan** (Butantan Snake Farm and Museum) ① *Av Dr Vital Brasil 1500, T011-3726 7222, Tue-Sun 0845-1615, www.butantan.gov.br, US$5, under-12s half price, under 7s free, Metrô Butantan (from 2012).*

③ Jardins & Avenida Paulista

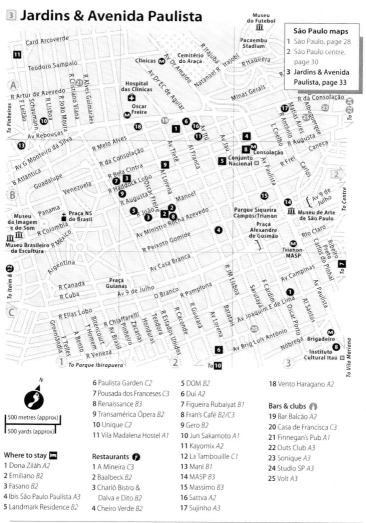

São Paulo maps
1 São Paulo, page 28
2 São Paulo centre, page 30
3 Jardins & Avenida Paulista, page 33

Where to stay 🛏
1 Dona Ziláh *A2*
2 Emiliano *B2*
3 Fasano *B2*
4 Ibis São Paulo Paulista *A3*
5 Landmark Residence *B2*
6 Paulista Garden *C2*
7 Pousada dos Franceses *C3*
8 Renaissance *B3*
9 Transamérica Ópera *B2*
10 Unique *C2*
11 Vila Madalena Hostel *A1*

Restaurants 🍴
1 A Mineira *C3*
2 Baalbeck *B2*
3 Charlô Bistro & Dalva e Dito *B2*
4 Cheiro Verde *B2*
5 DOM *B2*
6 Dui *A2*
7 Figueira Rubaiyat *B1*
8 Fran's Café *B2/C3*
9 Gero *B2*
10 Jun Sakamoto *A1*
11 Kayomix *A2*
12 La Tambouille *C1*
13 Mani *B1*
14 MASP *B3*
15 Massimo *B3*
16 Sattva *A2*
17 Sujinho *A3*
18 Vento Haragano *A2*

Bars & clubs 🍸
19 Bar Balcão *A2*
20 Casa de Francisca *C3*
21 Finnegan's Pub *A1*
22 Outs Club *A3*
23 Sonique *A3*
24 Studio SP *A3*
25 Volt *A3*

The insituto's collection of preserved snakes, spiders and scorpions was destroyed by fire in May 2010. The museum and vivarium are open to visitors. The **Museu de Arte Contemporâneo (MAC)** ① *T3091 3538, www.mac.usp.br, Tue-Sun 1000-1900, free,* with an important collection of Brazilian and European modern art, is in the Prédio Novo da Reitoria. Also here is the **Museu de Arqueologia e Etnologia** (MAE) ① *R Reitoria 1466, T3091 4905,* with Amazonian and ancient Mediterranean collections. Not far from the Butantã Institute, just inside Cidade Universitária, is the **Casa do Bandeirante** ① *Praça Monteiro Lobato, T3031 0920, Tue-Sun 0900-1700,* the reconstructed home of a 17th-century pioneer.

On the west bank of the Rio Pinheiros, just southeast of the Cidade Universitária, is the palatial **Jóquei Clube/Jockey Club** ① *Av Lineu de Paula Machado 1263, T2161 8300, www.jockeysp.com.br,* racecourse in the Cidade Jardim area. Take Butantã bus from República. Race meetings are held Monday and Thursday at 1930 and weekends at 1430. It has a **Museu do Turfe** ① *Tue-Sun, closed Sat-Sun mornings.*

Morumbi is a smart residential district due south of the Cidade Universitária. In the area are the state government building, **Palácio dos Bandeirantes** ① *Av Morumbi 4500,* the small, simple **Capela de Morumbi** ① *Av Morumbi 5387,* and the Morumbi stadium of São Paulo Football Club, which holds 100,000 people. Motor racing fans might like to visit the Morumbi cemetery, last resting place of Ayrton Senna; take 6291 bus to Rua Profesor Benedito Montenegro.

Museu da Fundação Maria Luisa e Oscar Americano ① *Av Morumbi 4077, Morumbi, T3742 0077, www.fundacaooscaramericano.org.br, Tue-Sun 1000-1730, US$4,* is a private collection of Brazilian and Portuguese art and furniture. The garden has fascinating paths, patios and plants; concerts are held on Sunday and courses through the week. It is close to the Palácio dos Bandeirantes.

Burle Marx Park ① *Av Dona Helena Pereira de Moraes 200, Morumbi, daily 0700-1900.* Designed by famous landscape designer Burle Marx, it has trails leading through the Mata Atlântica (Atlantic rainforest).

South of the Old Centre

Ibirapuera

The **Parque do Ibirapuera** ① *entrance on Av Pedro Álvares Cabral, daily 0600-1730,* was designed by Oscar Niemeyer and landscape artist Roberto Burle Marx for the city's fourth centenary in 1954. Within its 160 ha is the **Assembléia Legislativa** and a **planetarium** ① *T5575 5206, Sat, Sun 1200-1800, US$5.* After many years of refurbishment it now has state-of-the-art fittings. Buy tickets 30 minutes before the show. Also in the park is the **Museu de Arte Moderna** (MAM) ① *T5085 1300, www.mam.org.br, Tue-Sun 1000-1800, US$2.75,* with art exhibitions and sculpture garden (see Nuno Ramos' Craca – Barnacle). It has a great café restaurant and art shop. **Museu Afro-Brasileiro** ① *T5579 0593, Wed-Sun 1000-1800, free:* temporary exhibitions, theatre, dance and cinema spaces, photographs and panels devoted to exploring African Brazil. **Pavilhão Japonês** ① *T3573 6543, Sat, Sun 1000-1700, free except for exhibitions,* exhibition space showing works from Japanese and Japanese-Brazilian artists, designed by Japanese and built exclusively with materials from Japan. It is set in Japanese gardens and has a traditional tea house upstairs. Bicycles can be hired in the park, US$3 per hour. Buses to Ibirapuera, 574R from Paraíso Metrô station;

6364 from Praça da Bandeira; to Cidade Universitária 702U or 7181 from Praça da República. Every even-numbered year the **Bienal Internacional de São Paulo** (São Paulo Biennial) at Ibirapuera has the most important show of modern art in Latin America, usually in September.

Parque da Independência

In the suburb of Ipiranga, 5.5 km southeast of the city centre, the Parque da Independência contains the **Monumento à Independência**. Beneath the monument is the Imperial Chapel ① *Tue-Sun 1300-1700*, with the tomb of the first emperor, Dom Pedro I, and Empress Leopoldina. **Casa do Grito** ① *Tue-Sun 0930-1700*, the little house in which Dom Pedro I spent the night before his famous cry of Ipiranga, 'Independence or Death', is preserved in the park. The **Museu Paulista** ① *T6165 8000, Tue-Sun 0900-1645, US$1*, contains old maps, traditional furniture, collections of old coins, religious art and *indígena* ethnology. Behind the Museum is the **Horto Botânico** (**Ipiranga Botanical Garden**) and the **Jardim Francês** ① *Tue-Sun 0900-1700, getting there: take bus 478-P (Ipiranga-Pompéia for return) from Ana Rosa, or take bus 4612 from Praça da República.*

Parque do Estado (Jardim Botânico)

This large park, a long way south of the centre, at **Água Funda** ① *Av Miguel Estefano 3031-3687, T5573 6300, Wed-Sun 0900-1700, getting there: take Metrô to São Judas on the Jabaquara line, then take a bus*, contains the Jardim Botânico, with lakes and trees and places for picnics, and a very fine orchid farm worth seeing during November-December (orchid exhibitions in April and November).

São Paulo listings

For hotel and restaurant price codes and other relevant information, see page 11.

Where to stay

For both business and leisure, São Paulo has by far the best hotels in Brazil. The best area to stay is northeastern Jardins (also known as Cerqueria César), which is safe and well connected to the Metrô via Av Paulista. There are cheapies in the centre, but this is an undesirable area at night.

Jardins, Avenida Paulista and around
p32, map p33

$$$$ Emiliano, R Oscar Freire 384, T3069 4369, www.emiliano.com.br. Bright and beautifully designed, attention to detail and the best suites in the city. No pool but a relaxing small spa. Excellent Italian restaurant, location and service.

$$$$ Fasano, R Vittorio Fasano 88, T3896 4077, www.fasano.com.br. One of the world's great hotels with decor like a modernist gentleman's club designed by Armani, a fabulous pool and the best formal haute cuisine restaurant in Brazil. Excellently positioned in Jardins.

$$$$ Unique, Av Brigadeiro Luis Antônio 4700, Jardim Paulista, T3055 4700, www.hotel unique.com. The most ostentatious hotel in the country, an enormous half moon on concrete uprights with curving floors, circular windows and beautiful use of space and light. The bar on the top floor is São Paulo's answer to the LA Sky Bar and is always filled with the rich and famous after 2130.

$$$ Dona Ziláh, Al França 1621, Jardim Paulista, T3062 1444, www.zilah.com. Little pousada in a renovated colonial house, well maintained, decorated with a personal touch.

Excellent location, bike rental and generous breakfast included.

$$$ Formule 1 Paraíso, R Vergueiro 1571, T5085 5699, www.accorhotels.com.br. Another great value business-style hotel, apartments big enough for 3 make this an economic option for those in a group. Right next to Paraíso Metro in a safe area, a/c.

$$$ Ibis São Paulo Paulista, Av Paulista 2355, T3523 3000, www.accorhotels.com.br. Great value, modern business standard rooms with a/c, right on Paulista, cheaper Sat-Sun.

$$$ Paulista Garden, Al Lorena 21, T/F3885 8498, www.paulistagardenhotel.com.br. Small, simple rooms with a/c, cable TV and fridge, close to Ibirapuera Park.

$$$-$$ Pousada dos Franceses, R dos Franceses 100, Bela Vista, T3288 1592, www.pousadados franceses.com.br. Plain little pousada 10 mins' walk from Brigadeiro Metrô. dorms, doubles and singles, free internet, TV room, breakfast included.

$$$-$ Vila Madalena Hostel, R Francisco Leitão 686, T3034 4104, www.vilamadalena hostel.com. Price for double bed US$24-30 in dorms for 4 or 8. 15 mins from Clínicas Metrô, well-run, popular, arty hostel with good services, bikes for rent, internet and Wi-Fi.

$$-$ Casa Club, R Mourata Coelho 973, Vila Madalena, T3798 0051, www.casaclub.com.br. Tiny hostel with shared rooms that can be booked privately, one for women only. Previously a bar and retains its party atmosphere, Wi-Fi, restaurant.

$$-$ Sampa Hostel, R Girassol 519, Vila Madalena, T3031 6779, www.sampahostel.com.br. Dorms (US$20-25) and 2 private rooms which need booking in advance, convenient, with fan, breakfast, Wi-Fi.

● **Restaurants**

Jardins *p32, map p33*

Those on a budget can eat to their stomach's content in per kg places or, cheaper still, bakeries (*padarias*) There's one on almost every corner and they serve sandwiches, delicious Brazilian burgers made from decent meat and served with ham, egg, cheese or salad. They always have good coffee, juices, cakes and set lunches (*almoços*) for a very economical price. Most have a designated sitting area – either at the *padaria* bar or in an adjacent room. Juices are made from mineral or filtered water.

$$$ Charlô Bistro, R Barão de Capanema 440 (next to DOM), T3088 6790 (with another branch at the Jockey Club, Av Lineu de Paula Machado 1263, Cidade Jardim, T3034 3682). One of the premier VIP and old family haunts in the city run by a scion of one of the city's establishment families. Decked out in tribute to a Paris brasserie and with food to match.

$$$ DOM, R Barão de Capanema 549, T3088 0761. Jardins' evening restaurant of the moment – Alex Attala has won the coveted Veja best chef of the year award twice. Contemporary food, fusing Brazilian ingredients with French and Italian styles and served in a large modernist dining room.

$$$ Fasano, in Hotel Fasano (see Where to stay), T3896 4077. Long regarded as the leading gourmet restaurant in São Paulo. A huge choice of modern Italian and French cooking from chef Salvatore Loi. Diners have their own lowly lit booths in a magnificent dining room, exemplary wine list, formal dress.

$$$ Figueira Rubaiyat, R Haddock Lobo 1738, T3063 3888. The most interesting of the Rubaiyat restaurant group, supervised by Argentinian chef Francis Mallman. Very lively for Sun lunch, light and airy and under a huge tropical fig tree. The best meat is served at another restaurant in the chain, Baby Beef Rubaiyat, Av Brig Faria Lima 2954, T3078 9488.

$$$ Gero, R Haddock Lobo 1629, T3064 0005. Fasano's version of a French Bistrô a Côté, but serving pasta and light Italian. Ever so casual design; be prepared for a long wait at the bar alongside people who are there principally to be seen. Reservations are not accepted.

$$$ Jun Sakamoto, R Lisboa 55, T3088 6019. Japanese with a touch of French; superb fresh ingredients (some of it flown in especially from Asia and the USA).

$$$ La Tambouille, Av 9 de Julho 5925, Jardim Europa, T3079 6276. The favourite 'old money' Franco-Italian restaurant. Excellent wine list.

$$$ Massimo, Al Santos 1826, Cerqueira César, T3284 0311. One of São Paulo's longest established Italian restaurants serving Northern Italian food. Credit cards are not accepted, despite the costly price.

$$$ Vento Haragano, Av Rebouças 1001, T3083 4265. One of the city's best rodízios.

$$ A Mineira, Al Joaquim Eugénio de Lima 697, T3283 2349. Self-service Minas food by the kilo. Lots of choice. Cachaça and pudding included.

$$ Baalbeck, Al Lorena 1330, T3088 4820. Lebanese cooking vastly superior to its luncheonette setting. Great falafel.

$$ Fran's Café, Av Paulista 358, and throughout the city. Open 24 hrs, the Brazilian equivalent of Starbuck's but with proper coffee and light meals.

$$ Kayomix, R da Consolação 3215, T3082 2769. Brazilian Oriental fusions like salmon taratare with shimeji and shitake.

$$ Restaurante do MASP, Av Paulista 1578, T3253 2829. In the basement of the museum, reasonably priced standards like lasagna and stroganoff often with a garnish of live music.

$$ Sujinho, R da Consolação 2068, Consolação, T3256 8026. South American beef in large portions, other carnivorous options also available.

$ Cheiro Verde, R Peixoto Gomide 1413, T289 6853 (lunch only). Hearty veggie food, like vegetable crumble in gorgonzola sauce and pasta with buffalo mozarella and sun-dried tomato.

☻ Bars and clubs

The best places for nightlife are Itaim, Moema and Vila Olímpia, and Vila Madalena/

Pinheiros. Jardins' best bars are in the top hotels. Vila Olímpia, Itaim and Moema have a series of funky, smart bars overflowing onto the street, filled with an eclectic mix of after-workers, clubbers, singles and couples; all united by being under 40 and having money. These sit alongside imitation US and European club/lounge bars playing techno, hip hop and the like. The busiest streets for a bar wander are Rua Atílio Inocenti near the junction of Av Juscelino Kubitschek and Av Brigadeiro Faria Lima, Av Hélio Pellegrino and Rua Araguari, which runs behind it. Vila Madalena is younger still, more hippy-chic, but is the best part of town to hear live, Brazilian music and uniquely Brazilian close dances like Forró, as opposed to international club sounds. The liveliest streets are Aspicuelta and Girassol.

Jardins *p32, map p33*
Bar Balcão, R Dr Melo Alves 150, T3063 6091. After work meeting place, very popular with young professionals and media types who gather on either side of the long low wooden bar which winds its way around the room like a giant snake.

Finnegan's Pub, R Cristiano Viana 358, Pinheiros. One of São Paulo's various Irish bars, this one actually run by an Irishman, popular with ex-pats.

☻ Transport

São Paulo *p26, maps p28, p30 and p33*
Air From the international airport **Guarulhos** (also known as Cumbica), T6445 2945, there are airport taxis which charge US$65 on a ticket system (the taxi offices are outside Customs, 300 m down on the left; go to get your ticket then take your bags right back to the end of the taxi queue). Fares from the city to the airport are slightly less and vary from cab to cab. Various **Emtubus** city buses (www.emtu.sp.gov.br) run from Guarulhos to Praça da República, Congonhas airport, Barra Funda terminal, Itaim Bibi and a circuit of

hotels, US$19; also to Tatuapé Metrô station, US$2.50. **Pássaro Marron** airport bus service, T0800-770 7995, Mon-Fri 0700-1900, weekends T2445-2430, www.airport buservice.com.br, also run buses between Guarulhos, the city centre, rodoviárias, Congonhas airport, Avenida Paulista and Jardins hotels, etc; frequent service 0500-2330 (0430 to Tietê), US$12.50. From **Congonhas airport**, there are about 400 flights a week to Rio. Taxi Congonhas airport-Jardins is US$19.

Airport information Money exchanges, in the arrivals hall, Guarulhos, 0800-2200 daily. Post office on the 3rd floor of Asa A. See Arriving in São Paolo, page 26, for the tourist office.

Bus City buses are run by **SP Trans**, www.sptrans.com.br. You can work out your route on the planner on the bus company's website and on Google maps, which mark bus stops. These maps, plus those on the Metrô and **CPTM** websites (see below) will give you a good coverage of the city. Even if you do not speak Portuguese they are fairly self-explanatory. Local transport maps are also available at stations and depots. Some city bus routes are run by trolley buses. City bus fare is US$1.65.

Metrô The best and cheapest way to get around São Paulo is on the excellent metrô system, daily 0500-2400, www.metro.sp.gov.br, with a clear journey planner and information in Portuguese and English. It is clean, safe, cheap and efficient and has 5 main lines. It is integrated with the overground **CPTM** (Companhia Paulista de Trens Metropolitanos), www.cptm.sp.gov.br, an urban light railway which serves to extend the metrô along the margins of the Tietê and Pinheiros rivers and to the outer city suburbs. There are 6 lines, numbers 7 to 12, which are colour-coded like the metrô. Information T0800-055 0121. Fare US$1.65; backpacks are allowed. Combined bus and Metrô ticket are available, US$2.55. The *bilhete único* integrates bus, metro and light railway in a single, rechargeable plastic swipe card. US$2.55 serves for 1 metro or CPTM journey and 3 bus journeys within the space of 3 hrs (1 unit). Swipe cards can be bought at metro stations. The initial minimum charge is equivalent to 5 units. Swipe cards can be bought at thousands of authorised outlets, including SP Trans' own shops (eg Praça da Sé 188, R Augusta 449), metro stations, newsstands, lottery shops, etc.

Taxi Taxis display cards of actual tariffs in the window (starting price US$4). There are ordinary taxis, which are hailed on the street, or at taxi stations such as Praça da República, radio taxis and deluxe taxis. For **Radio Taxis**, which are more expensive but involve fewer hassles, **Central Radio Táxi**, T3035 0404, www.centralradiotaxi.com; **São Paulo Rádio Táxi**, T5073 2814. Visit www.taxisp.com.br for a list or look in the phone book; calls are not accepted from public phones.

Contents

Footprint features

The Amazon

Amapá and Pará

Sometimes called Brazilian Guyana, the isolated border state of Amapá was once exploited for its natural resources and suffered from heavy deforestation. However, efforts are now being made towards sustainable development. Located near the French territory of Guyane, with its cheap air links to Paris, it is another good port of entry into northern Brazil. Tourist infrastructure outside the provincial riverside capital of Macapá is negligible. The state is a quarter of the size of France and has a population of just under half a million. Pará is just across the river from Amapá – a distance that would span Switzerland. In the 1990s, the state capital, Belém, was dangerous and down at heel, but extensive refurbishment in the last decade has transformed it into an attractive colonial city. The state itself is barely aware of the existence of tourists. Although there are many beautiful natural sights, such as the vast river island of Marajó in the Amazon delta and the Amazônia National Park on the River Tapajós, infrastructure is poor, with no jungle lodges at all in the extensive rainforests. While areas north of the Amazon have been afforded at least nominal protection since 2006, in the south of the state rapid deforestation is making space for vast soya plantations. Santarém, a quiet little town at the junction of the Tapajós and Amazon rivers, is the world's largest soya-export port. Thankfully ecotourism is gradually catching on here: a few tour companies offer trips to the river beaches at Alter do Chao and the failed rubber plantation towns of Belterra and Fordlândia – set up by Henry Ford in the early 20th century. Monte Alegre, whose caves have revealed evidence of a significant pre-Columbian Amazon culture, are a day's boat ride away upstream. Travel in Pará takes time (as it does anywhere in the Amazon) and the more isolated parts of the state are often linked only by boat and air.

Macapá → *For listings, see pages 58-70. Phone code: 096. Population: 284,000.*

The capital of Amapá is a pleasant city on the banks of the northern channel of the Amazon delta. It has an impressive fortress as well as a monument to the equator, which divides the city. There is a museum detailing the research being carried out in the rainforest and at nearby Curiaú, a village originally formed by escaped slaves.

The town was founded around the first Forte de São José do Macapá, built in 1688. In 1751 more settlers from the Azores arrived to defend the region from Dutch, English and French invasions and the *aldea* became a *vila* in 1758. Many slaves were later brought from Africa for the construction of the fort.

Arriving in Macapá
Getting there The **airport** ① *R Hildemar Maia, 3 km from the centre, T096-3223 4087*, receives flights from Belém, Brasília, Foz do Iguaçu, Rio de Janeiro, São Paulo, São Luís, Fortaleza, Marabá and Cayenne (Guyane). Taxis to the centre cost around US$7.

Buses arrive at the new **rodoviária** ① *on the BR-156, 3 km north of Macapá*. Buses from Oiapoque pass through the city centre after a long and uncomfortable journey over mainly unsurfaced roads. This journey can take even longer during the rainy season (January to May). Boats from Belém and Santarém arrive at nearby Porto Santana, which is linked to Macapá by bus or taxi. ►► *See Transport, page 66.*

Macapá

Where to stay
Atalanta 1
Ceta Ecotel 8
Frota Palace 3
Gloria 4
Holliday 9
Macapá 5
Mercúrio 6
Pousada Ekinox 2
Santo Antônio 7
Vista Amazônica 10

Restaurants
Bom Paladar Kilo's 3
Cantinho Baiano 2
Chalé 1
Divina Arte 5
Divina Gula 6
Flora 7
Sarney 8

Getting around There is an air-taxi service to some towns, however, most are linked by the trucks, buses and community minibuses, which leave from the new *rodoviária*. Buses to other parts of the city leave from a bus station near the fort. The centre and the waterfront are easily explored on foot.

Tourist information SETUR ① *Av Binga Uchôa 29, T096-3212 5335, www.setur.ap.gov.br, Mon-Fri 1000-1800*, also has a branch at the airport. For information on national parks, contact Instituto Chico Mendes de Conservação da Biodiversidade (ICMBio) ① *www.icmbio.gov.br*. The website www.macapaturismo.com.br is also useful.

Places in Macapá

Each brick of the **Fortaleza de São José do Macapá**, built between 1764 and 1782, was brought from Portugal as ballast. Fifty iron cannon still remain and there is a museum. The *fortaleza* is used for concerts, exhibitions and colourful festivities on the anniversary of the city's founding on 4 February. **São José cathedral**, inaugurated by the Jesuits in 1761, is the city's oldest landmark. The **Centro de Cultura Negra** ① *R General Rondon*, has a museum and holds frequent events. The **Museu do Desenvolvimento Sustentável** ① *Av Feliciano Coelho 1509, Tue-Fri 0830-1200, 1500-1800, Mon and Sat 1500-1800*, exhibits research on sustainable development and traditional community life in Amazônia. The museum shop sells arts and crafts.

The riverfront has been landscaped with trees, lawns and paths and is a very pleasant place for an evening stroll. The **Complexo Beira Rio** has food and drink kiosks and a lively atmosphere. The recently rebuilt *trapiche* (pier) is a lovely spot for savouring the cool of the evening breeze, or watching the sun rise over the Amazon.

There is a monument to the equator, **Marco Zero** (take Fazendinha bus from Avenida Mendonça Furtado). The equator also divides the enormous football stadium nearby, aptly named O Zerão. The Sambódromo stadium is located nearby. South of here are the **botanical gardens** ① *Rodovia Juscelino Kubitschek, Km 12, Tue-Sun 0900-1700*.

Excursions from Macapá

Some 16 km from the centre, **Fazendinha** is a popular local beach, which is very busy on Sunday and has many seafood restaurants. **Curiaú**, 8 km from Macapá, is inhabited by the descendants of African slaves, who have maintained many of the customs of their ancestors. They are analogous to the Bush Negroes of Suriname, making the village the only one of its kind in Brazil. It is popular at weekends for dancing and swimming. The surrounding area is an environmental reserve with many water buffalo.

North of Macapá → *For listings, see pages 58-70.*

North of Macapá the road divides at **Porto Grande**, and a branch heads northwest to **Serra do Navio** where manganese extraction has now ended (Hotel Serra do Navio and several bars and restaurants). The BR-156 continues north, passing the turnings for two jungle hotels. The paved road goes as far as **Ferreira Gomes** on the shores of the Rio Araguari. Further on is **Amapá**, formerly the territorial capital and location of a Second World War American airbase. There are a few hotels. Beyond Amapá is **Calçoene**, with a government-owned hotel that serves expensive food in an adjoining canteen; very cheap

The river sea

Many people imagine the Amazon as a single river but, in reality, it is a huge network of rivers extending into nine countries. Before the Andes were formed, some 15 million years ago, the Amazon flowed west into the Pacific. However, as the crash of continental plates pushed up the mountains, the river was cut off from its ocean and became a vast inland sea, hemmed in by the Guiana Shield to the east. Over millions of years this sea eroded the ancient conglomerate shield, until it eventually burst through into the Atlantic. It left behind a vast filigree of veins that today make up the Amazon river system, populated by prehistoric, air-breathing fish like the pirarucu, and unique freshwater species such as the Amazon stingrays (*Potamatrygonidae*), whose closest relatives still live in the Pacific.

accommodation is also advertised in a café on the Oiapoque road. North of Calçoene a road branches west to **Lourenço**, whose goldfields still produce even after decades of prospecting. The main road continues north across the Rio Caciporé and on to the border with French Guyane at **Oiapoque**, on the river of the same name.

Oiapoque

This is a ramshackle little gold-mining town with dirt streets lined with little guesthouses, spit-and-sawdust bars and shops buying the precious metal by the gram. It lies 90 km inland from **Cabo Orange**, Brazil's northernmost point on the Atlantic Coast and the site of one of its wildest and remotest national parks. Access to the park is very difficult although guides can sometimes be arranged through the boatmen on the river docks in Oiapoque.

Oiapoque town has its share of contraband, illegal migration and drug trafficking and can be a little rough; visitors should be cautious, especially late at night. With the building of the road between St-Georges Oyapock and Cayenne, the town has become a popular spot for French Guianan weekenders, most of them single men and in search of more than a drink. The **Cachoeira Grande Roche** rapids can be visited, upstream along the Oiapoque river, where it is possible to swim, US$30 by motor boat. The **Associação dos Povos Indigenous Brazilians de Oiapoque**, in front of the Banco do Brasil, provides information about the indigenous peoples that live in the area, and the indigenous Uaçá reserve.

The road construction has led to significant environmental damage with much deforestation along the Brazilian side of the road in Amapá, and Brazilian *garimpeiros* and hunters illegally flooding into Guyane have been causing havoc in pristine forests.

Belém → *For listings, see pages 58-70. Phone code: 091. Population: 1.3 million.*

Belém do Pará is the great port of the eastern Amazon. The city received an extensive facelift in the new millennium and is now a very pleasant capital with much of cultural interest – with streets of freshly painted, impressive 19th-century buildings from the rubber boom era and one of Latin America's liveliest contemporary music scenes. The reforms included opening up the waterfront and converting the derelict docks into a breezy promenade, which leads to one of Brazil's more colourful markets – Ver o Peso.

Albery Albuquerque recommends

There is no one quite like Albery Albuquerque, www.myspace.com/alberyalbuquerque. He makes music from the rainforest by spending months recording birds and wild animals in the heart of the Amazon and precisely reproducing their calls with keyboard, voice and stringed instruments within his complex instrumental music. Here are his recommendations for what to do in Belém:

→ Take a taxi to Ver-o-Rio (Pedro Alvares Cabras near to Moinho Santa Rosa) for sunset. The views out over the river and the colours in the sky are magical.

→ If you have only a little time in Belém be sure to visit Cotijuba island for a taste of the forest and a sense of the size and magnificence of Amazonian nature.

Belém is a good base for boat trips along the river – either as cruises or public transport to Santarém, Manaus and beyond. An archipelago of beautiful, unspoilt tropical river islands lies a short boat trip offshore. The largest, Marajó, is as big as Denmark. With mean temperatures of 26°C, Belém is hot, but frequent showers and a prevailing breeze freshen the streets. The city has its fair share of crime and is prone to gang violence. Take sensible precautions, especially at night.

Arriving in Belém

Getting there Val-de-Cans international airport ① *Av Júlio César s/n, 12 km from the city, T091-3210 6000*, receives flights from the, Caribbean, the Guianas and the major Brazilian capitals. The airport bus 'Perpétuo Socorro-Telégrafo' or 'Icoaraci' runs every 15 minutes to the Prefeitura on Praça Felipe Patroni (US$1.50, allow 40 minutes). A taxi from the airport into town costs US$18. Ordinary taxis are cheaper than co-operatives, buy ticket in advance in departures side of airport. There are ATMs in the terminal, tourist information, cafés and car rental.

There are road connections from São Luís and the northeastern coast as well as a three-day bus link from São Paulo via Brasília. Interstate buses arrive at the **rodoviária** ① *end of Av Gov José Malcher, 3 km from the centre*. There are showers (US$0.10), a good snack bar, and agencies with information and tickets for riverboats. Buses to the centre cost US$0.50; taxis charge US$5-7. At the *rodoviária* you are given a ticket with the taxi's number on it; threaten to go to the authorities if the driver tries to overcharge.

Boats arrive at the port from Macapá, Manaus and Santarém as well as other parts of the Amazon region and delta. ▶▶ *See Transport, page 67.*

Getting around The city centre is easily explored on foot. City buses and taxis run to all the sites of interest and to transport hubs away from the centre.

Tourist information Paratur ① *Praça Waldemar Henrique, Reduto, on the waterfront, T091-3224 9493, www.paraturismo.pa.gov.br*, has information on the state and city. Some staff speak English and can book hotels and tours to Marajó island. For information on national parks contact the **Instituto Chico Mendes de Conservação da Biodiversidade (ICMBio)** ① *www.icmbio.gov.br.* The website www.belemonline.com.br is also useful.

Background

Established in 1616 because of its strategic position, Belém soon became the centre for slaving expeditions into the Amazon Basin. The Portuguese of Pará, together with those of Maranhão, treated the indigenous Brazilians abominably. Their isolation from the longer-established colonies allowed both places to become relatively lawless. In 1655, the Jesuits, under Antônio Vieira, attempted to lessen the abuses, while enticing the indigenous Brazilians to descend to the *aldeias* around Belém. This unfortunately led to further misery when smallpox spread from the south, striking the Pará *aldeias* in the 1660s.

Soon after Brazil's Independence, the Revolta da Cabanagem, a rebellion by the poor blacks, indigenous Brazilians and mixed-race *cabanos*, was led against the Portuguese-born class that dominated the economy. The movement came to an end in 1840 when the *cabanos* finally surrendered, but the worst years of violence were 1835-1836. Some estimates say 30,000 were killed. The state's strategic location once again became important during the Second World War, when Belém was used as an airbase by the Americans to hunt German submarines in the Atlantic.

Places in Belém

Belém used to be called the 'city of mango trees' and there are still many such trees remaining. There are some fine squares and restored historic buildings set along broad

① **Belém orientation**

Belém maps
1 Belém orientation, page 45
2 Belém centre, page 46

avenues. The largest square is the **Praça da República**, where there are free afternoon concerts; the main business and shopping area is along the wide Avenida Presidente Vargas, leading to the river, and the narrow streets which parallel it.

The recently restored neoclassical **Teatro da Paz** ⓘ *R da Paz, T091-4009 8750, www.theatrodapaz.com.br, Mon-Fri 0900-1700, Sat 0900-1200, tours US$3,* (1878), is one of the largest theatres in Brazil and its handsome ballrooms, polished floors, extensive murals and paintings and overall opulence are every bit as impressive as those of the theatre's more famous counterpart in Manaus. It was inspired by the Scala in Milan and is stuffed with imported materials from Europe – an iron frame built in England, Italian

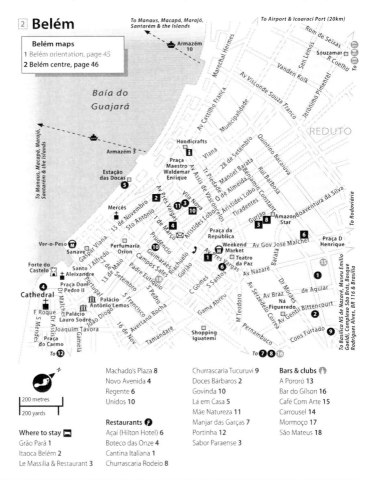

2 Belém

Belém maps
1 Belém orientation, page 45
2 Belém centre, page 46

Where to stay 🛏
Grão Pará **1**
Itaoca Belém **2**
Le Massilia & Restaurant **3**
Machado's Plaza **8**
Novo Avenida **4**
Regente **6**
Unidos **10**

Restaurants 🍴
Açaí (Hilton Hotel) **6**
Boteco das Onze **4**
Cantina Italiana **1**
Churrascaria Rodeio **8**
Churrascaria Tucuruvi **9**
Doces Bárbaros **2**
Govinda **10**
Lá em Casa **5**
Mãe Natureza **11**
Manjar das Garças **7**
Portinha **12**
Sabor Paraense **3**

Bars & clubs 🍸
A Pororó **13**
Bar do Gilson **16**
Café Com Arte **15**
Carrousel **14**
Mormoço **17**
São Mateus **18**

marble, French bronzes and a Portuguese mosaic stone floor. The auditorium once featured a magnificent ceiling painting by Domenico de Angelis (see the Pálacio Lauro Sodré and the cathedral below) who also worked in the Teatro Amazonas in Manaus, which crumbled and fell to the floor only decades after it was painted. The theatre stages performances by national and international stars, and offers free concerts and shows.

West of here, at the **Estação das Docas**, the abandoned warehouses and quays of the port have been restored into a waterfront complex with an air-conditioned interior with a gallery of cafés, restaurants and boutiques. It's a great place to come in the late afternoon when the sun is golden over the Baía do Guajará and locals promenade along the cobbles under the towering 19th-century cranes. There are three converted warehouses in the Estação das Docas – each a 'boulevard'. The Boulevard das Artes contains the **Cervejaria Amazon** (brewery), with good beer and simple meals, an archaeological museum and arts and crafts shops. The Boulevard de Gastronomia has smart restaurants and the five-star **Cairu** ice cream parlour (try *açaí* or the *pavê de capuaçu*). In the Boulevard das Feiras there are trade fairs. Live music is transported between the boulevards on a moving stage. There are also ATMs and an internet café within the complex.

Heading south, the 17th-century **Mercês church** (1640) is the oldest in Belém. It forms part of an architectural group known as the Mercedário, the rest of which was heavily damaged by fire in 1978 and has now been restored.

Near the church, the Belém market, known as **Ver-o-Peso** ① *Blvd Castilhos França 27, T091-3212 0549*, was the Portuguese Posto Fiscal, where goods were weighed to gauge taxes due, hence the name: 'see the weight'. Inside are a flurry of stalls selling all manner of items – herbal remedies, Brazil nuts, açaí, bead jewellery, African-Brazilian religious charms, incense and, in the main gallery, scores of tiled slabs covered with bizarre river fish – from piraiba as big as a man to foot-long armour-plated cat fish. You can see them being unloaded at around 0530, together with hundreds of baskets of açaí. A colourful, if dirty, dock for fishing boats lies immediately upriver from the market and whole area swarms with people, including armed thieves and pickpockets.

Around Praça Dom Pedro II is a cluster of interesting buildings. The **Palácio Lauro Sodré** and **Museu do Estado do Pará** ① *Praça Dom Pedro II, T091-3225 3853, Mon-Fri 0900-1800, Sat 1000-1800*, is a gracious 18th-century Italianate building. It contains Brazil's largest framed painting, *The Conquest of Amazônia*, by Domenico de Angelis. The building was the work of the Italian architect António Landi, who also designed the cathedral, and was the administrative seat of the colonial government. During the rubber boom many new decorative features were added. Also on Praça Dom Pedro II is the **Palácio Antônio Lemos**, which houses the **Museu de Arte de Belém** as well as the **Prefeitura** ① *Tue-Fri 0900-1200, 1400-1800, Sat and Sun 0900-1300*. It was originally built as the Palácio Municipal between 1868 and 1883, and is a fine example of the Imperial neoclassical style. In the downstairs rooms there are old views of Belém; upstairs, the historic rooms, beautifully renovated, contain furniture and paintings, which are all well explained.

The **cathedral** ① *Praça Frei Caetano Brandão, Mon 1500-1800, Tue-Fri 0800-1100, 1530-1800* (1748), is also neoclassical, and contains a series of brilliantly coloured paintings by the Italian artist Domenico de Angelis – famous for his work on the Teatro Amazonas in Manaus, but whose first visit to the Amazon was to Belem in 1884 to paint this cathedral and the Teatro da Paz. Directly opposite is the restored 18th-century **Santo Alexandre church** ① *Praça Frei Caetano Brandão s/n, Mon 1500-1800, Tue-Fri 0800-1100, 1530-1800*, with a

The Festival of Candles

Our Lady of Nazareth has been celebrated with syncretistic festivals in Spain and Portugal since an image of the Virgin arrived in the monastery of Caulina in Spain in AD 361. It lay buried for many years under Saint Bartholomew's peak in Caulina, in protection against the Muslim invaders, but was recovered and taken to Portugal in 1119 where the effigy was said to have been the source of countless miracles.

The effigy in the Basílica de Nossa Senhora de Nazaré church was discovered by Plácido José de Souza, a caboclo, in 1700, buried in mud on an igarapé near Belém. De Souza built a chapel for the image, and over the following century the statue became associated with miracles in Pará; so much so that it began to be carried around the streets in veneration every October. In 1793, the Vatican authorized the first official processions in Belém, in celebration of Our Lady of Nazareth. Today the effigy forms the focus of the largest festival in this part of northern Brazil, the Círio de Nazaré.

On the second Sunday in October, a procession carries a copy of the Virgin's image from the Basílica to the cathedral, in a procession which attracts up to a million visitors. On the Monday, two weeks later, the image is returned to its usual resting place. Alongside the Sunday procession there's a lively festival known as the **Carnabelém**, which attracts many major Brazilian artists and musicians; carnival performers attend, along with an increasing contingent of international artists. There is a Círio museum in the crypt of the Basílica, enter at the right side of the church; free entry. For dates check with Paratur (see page 44).

---

fabulous rococo pediment and fine woodcarving. This was once the Jesuit headquarters in Belém – where Father Antonio Vieira (see box opposite) would have preached his hellfire sermons denouncing the indigenous slave trade; inciting the wrath of the locals, Pombal and eventually contributing to the disestablishment of the order.

Also in the old town is the **Forte do Castelo** ① *Praça Frei Caetano Brandão 117, T091- 3223 0041, daily 0800-2300*, which was rebuilt in 1878. The fort overlooks the confluence of the Rio Guamá and the Baía do Guajará and was where the Portuguese first set up their defences. There is a good restaurant, the **Boteco Onze**, where you can watch the sunset (entry US$1, drinks and *salgadinhos* served on the ramparts from 1800). At the square on the waterfront below the fort, the açaí berries are landed nightly at 2300, after being picked in the jungle. Açaí berries, ground up with sugar and mixed with manioc, are a staple food in the region.

East of the centre, the **Basílica de Nossa Senhora de Nazaré** ① *Praça Justo Chermont, Av Magalhães Barata, Mon-Sat 0500-1130, 1400-2000, Sun 0545-1130, 1430-2000*, was built in 1909 from rubber wealth. It is romanesque in style and has beautiful marble and stained-glass windows. The *basílica* feels very tranquil and sacred, especially when empty. A museum here showcases the Círio de Nazaré. The Nossa Senhora de Nazaré sits illuminated in a shrine in the sacristy. See also box above.

The botanic gardens, **Bosque Rodrigues Alves** ① *Av Almirante Barroso 2305, T091-3226 2308, Tue-Sun 0800-1700*, is a 16-ha public garden (really a preserved area of original flora), with a small animal collection. To get there, take the yellow bus marked 'Souza' or 'Cidade Nova' (any number), 30 minutes from Ver-o-Peso market, or from the

The Jesuits and the slave trade

Cristobal de Acuna, a Jesuit who visited the Amazon in the 1620s, describes an incredible density of villages along the lower Amazon. He writes of the happy and abundant life of the Omagua people, the largest of the tribal nations, who lived in large towns with handsome houses, fired pottery as fine as any in Europe, baked bread, wove cotton and farmed turtles. Within 100 years of his visit they and all the slaves of the lower Amazon nations were killed and their cultures and achievements lost for ever.

They were lost to 'Red Gold', the little-known Amazon slave trade. The indigenous people were rounded up in droves and brought to São Luís and Belém to farm the burgeoning sugar plantations where they were forced to live in appalling conditions and work until they died. Only the Jesuits sought to abate this human traffic. They had long defended the Guaraní in southern Brazil by persuading them to move into settlements organized along European lines, which were known as reductions or *aldeias*. They were determined to do the same in the Amazon. Their leader, Antônio Viera, berated the people of São Luís and Belém with hellfire sermons: "What is a human soul worth to Satan?" he asked; "There is no market on earth where the devil can get them more cheaply than right here in our own land … What a cheap market! An Indian for a soul! Christians, nobles," he begged "break the chains of injustice and free those whom you hold captive and oppressed!"

Viera was successful… for a while. The captives would be sent to Jesuit reductions from where they would be on loan to plantation owners for six months each year. The locals were certainly treated with less cruelty by the Jesuits. However, the Order were, in effect, equally responsible for the loss of indigenous life and culture. The reductions were breeding grounds for European disease and the native people were forced to completely abandon their religious and social practices. And when the Order was forced to leave Iberian America after a campaign against them by Portugal's Marquis de Pombal, the indigenous people who had been under their charge were enslaved and treated with renewed viciousness.

A typical Jesuit reduction was rectangular and built around a large *praça de armas*. To the rear of the plaza stood the church. On one side of the church was the cemetery and on the other the *claustro*, where the Jesuits themselves lived and studied. Near this were the workshops in which the works of art were produced. Behind the church were the gardens. Around the other sides of the plaza were the houses in which the Indians lived. The streets between the buildings were at right angles to each other and the settlement could easily be expanded along this plan. Chapels were built on the sides of the plaza. Other buildings included the *cabildo* (the municipal building of the indigenous people), the *cotiguazu* (a house for widows), a prison, a hospital and an inn for visitors.

cathedral. The **Museu Emílio Goeldi** ① *Av Magalhães Barata 376, Tue-Thu 0900-1200, 1400-1700, Fri 0900-1200, Sat and Sun 0900-1700, US$1,* takes up an entire city block and consists of the museum proper (with a fine collection of indigenous Marajó pottery and an excellent exhibition of Mebengokre tribal lifestyle), a rather sad zoo and botanical exhibits including Victoria Régia lilies. Buses run from the cathedral.

The **Murucutu** ruins, an old Jesuit foundation, are reached by the Ceará bus from Praça da República; entry is via an unmarked door on the right of the Ceará bus station.

Around Belém → *For listings, see pages 58-70.*

A *foca* (passenger ferry) to the small town of **Barcarena** ① *daily departures from Ver-o-Peso, but best Tue-Fri, US$1*, makes an interesting half-day trip. A return trip on the ferry from Ver-o-Peso to Icaoraci provides a good view of the river. Several restaurants here serve excellent seafood; you can eat shrimp and drink coconut water and appreciate the breeze coming off the river. **Icaoraci** is 20 km east of the city and is well known as a centre of ceramic production. The pottery is in Marajóara and Tapajonica style. Artisans are friendly and helpful, will accept commissions and send purchases overseas. A bus from Avenida Presidente Vargas in Belém runs to Icoaraci.

The nearest beach to Belém is at **Outeiro** (35 km), on an island near Icoaraci. It takes about an hour by bus and ferry (the bus may be caught near the **Maloca**, an indigenous- style hut near the docks that serves as a nightclub). A bus from Icoaraci to Outeiro takes 30 minutes.

Salinópolis

Some 223 km from Belém, at the extreme eastern end of the Amazon delta, this seaside resort has many small places where you can eat and drink at night by the waterfront. There is a fine sandy beach nearby (buses and cars drive onto the beach), but the water is murky. It is a peaceful place mid-week but very busy at weekends and in high season and is at its peak during the holiday month of July.

Atalaia, an island opposite Salinópolis, is pleasant and can be reached by taxi (US$6) or by boat. Salinópolis is four hours from Belém by bus on a good road, US$6.

The little riverside village of **Tomé-Açu**, south of Belém on the Rio Acará-Mirim, affords a view of life on a smaller river than the Amazon. Three buses a day run from Belém, US$8. The **Hotel Las Vegas** has a friendly owner, Fernando. The boat back to Belém on Sunday leaves at 1100, arriving 1800, US$5.

Islands around Belém

The mouth of the Amazon, formed by the confluence of that river in the north and the Tocantins in front of Belém, is dotted with islands and mangrove lined backwaters. There are 27 islands around Belém; the largest of which, **Marajó** (see below), is as big as Switzerland. Many islands can be visited on a day trip from the capital, others are a longer haul. Most are lined with long beaches of fine sand broken by strands of clay and dark stones heavy with iron ores. The water that washes them looks as expansive as an ocean, stretching to a vast horizon, but even out in what is geographically the Atlantic, it is fresh water and brown.

Ilha do Cotijuba, www.cotijuba.com, and the more built-up **Ilha do Mosqueiro**, www.mosqueiro.com.br, are reachable from Belém in a couple of hours. Both have a number of *pousadas* and small restaurants, stretches of forest and, on Cotijuba, gorgeous beaches. The islands get very crowded at Christmas and during Carnaval. The **Ilha da Mexiana** in the Marajó archipelago is more remote and less visited.

Boats run to Cotijuba from the docks in Belém (especially at the weekends), however, the quickest way to reach all the islands is from the port in **Icoaraci**, 20 km north of Belém

(30 minutes bus ride from the *rodoviária* or from near the Ver-o-Peso market; taxi US$25). There are at least four boats a day from here to Cotijuba; the first at 0900. Others only leave when full. The fastest take 20 minutes, the slowest one hour.

Mosqueiro is connected to the mainland by road. At least four buses a day leave from the *rodoviária* taking around 90 minutes to get to the main towns (Praia do Paraíso, Carandaduba and Vila Mosqueiro). There are no banks on any of these islands, so bring cash from Belém.

Ilha de Maiandeua and Vila do Algodoal

This sandy estuarine island with long sweeping beaches is more commonly known by the name of its principal town, Vila do Algodoal – a small-scale traveller resort very popular with French backpackers. The island is a semi-protected area at the junction of the sea, the Amazon and the Rio Maracanã. It is very tranquil and has sand dunes, small lakes and a number of isolated beaches lapped by an Atlantic heavy with the silt of the Amazon. The main town is tiny with a cluster of sandy streets lined with little houses, many of them *pousadas*, and fronted by a muddy beach, the Praia Caixa d'Agua. Donkey carts connect it with the island's other beaches, which include (running north and clockwise from Algodoal town), **Farol** (separated from Algodoal by a fast-flowing estuary and with flat tidal sands), and its continuation, the 14-km-long **Princesa** (with dunes, the best swimming and many of the cheap beach *pousadas*), **Fortalezinha** (some 20 km from Algodoal, with grey sands and weak waves, also reached across an estuarine inlet, but with with dangerously strong currents – cross on a ferry only), **Mococa** (around 23 km from Algodoal and with sharp stones and a small fishing community) and, on the other side of the bay from Algodoal town (reachable by boat – 30 minutes), **Marudá** (muddy and with a small town) and to its north **Crispim** (which has beach bars, dunes, and good windsurfing and which is very popular with Paraenses at weekends). All accommodation is low-key and simple. Be wary of stingrays on the beaches – especially in muddier areas – and of strong rip tides, sharks and strong waves on the beaches beyond Mococa – notably Enseada do Costeiro.

Buses run from Belém to Marudá town (2-3 hours, US$7, from Belém *rodoviária* from where you catch a ferry (30 minutes, US$3, around five ferries a day, last at 1700). There are onward bus connections from Marudá to Salinópolis and from there south to Maranhão. It is easy to find a room on arrival, except during weekends and holidays. There are no banks or ATMs in Algodoal. For more information see www.algodoal.com.br.

Ilha de Marajó

The largest island near Belém is also the largest riverine island in the world (although some claim that as it abuts the Atlantic the title belongs to Bananal in Tocantins). Like the rest of the Amazon, Marajó is partly flooded in the rainy season between January and June. The island is home to feral water buffalo, which can be seen in large numbers; they are said to have swum ashore after a shipwreck. Many are now farmed and Marajó is famous throughout Brazil for its *mozarela* cheese. The island's police force use the buffalo instead of horses to get around the beaches. The island is also home to numerous bird species, including thousands of roseate spoonbills, and black caiman, river turtles and other wildlife. There is good **birdwatching** on the fazendas, especially on **Fazenda Bom Jesus**, 5 km from Soure. This *fazenda*, owned by local matriarch Eva Abufaiad, has a delightful colonial chapel on over 6000 ha of land, and has rehabilitated much of its land for wildlife; a visit here is a real delight. Visits are easily organized through the Casarão da Amazônia (see page 60).

Visiting Ilha de Marajó A ferry from **Belém** sails twice daily (once daily at weekends), from the Armazem 10 dock in town (US$5). Boats also run from **Porto de Icoaraci**, 20 km north of Belém (30 minutes bus ride from the *rodoviária* or from near the Ver-o-Peso market; taxi US$25). Boats take three hours for the 30 km crossing to the island's main arrival point, **Porto de Camará** (20 km south of Salvaterra). From here, small craft await to transfer passengers to Salvaterra village (US$12, 30 minutes), Soure (US$14, 40 minutes, including a ferry crossing) or Praia de Joanes (US$4, 15 minutes). Each is clearly marked with the destination. There is also a taxi-plane service direct to Soure from Belém. The capital has a **Banco do Brasil** ATM, but this is unreliable. Changing money is only possible at very poor rates. There is internet in both Soure and Salvaterra. Take plenty of insect repellent. Bicycles and horses can be rented in both Slavaterra and Soure for around US$1/US$10 per hour respectively, to explore beaches and the interior of the island.

Background Marajo was was the site of the pre-Columbian **Marajóaras** civilization, celebrated for its ceramics, beautiful replicas of which can be bought from artisans in Soure. It is also a centre for candomble. Many of the communities here are descended from Africans who escaped slavery in Belém and fled to the forest to found their own villages or *quilombos*. A number of beaches around Soure are sacred candomble sites. The *quilombolas* did not remain altogether free of slavery, however. As Marajo was settled ranchers laid claim to the land, and much of the territory around Soure and Salvaterra which was originally community land is now privately owned. According to the news agency Brasil de Fato (www.brasildefato.com.br), many of the *quilombolas* are employed, and a system of semi-debt peonage – where their wages are offset against the cost of their rent and accommodation – is organized in such a way that they can never earn enough to pay off their employers. In 2007 the Ministry of Work and Employment freed a number of people from such slavery on the fazenda Santa Maria. Other *fazendas* – including Bom Jesus – stand accused of having their farm hands impede access to roads, including the PA-154 state road linking the *quilombo* community of Caju-Una with Soure.

Places on Ilha de Marajó The capital of Marajó is **Soure** (with a handful of restaurants, crafts shops and one of the island's best *pousadas*), with the other main town being **Salvaterra** (fine beaches and more choice of accommodation); both are on the eastern side of the island, which has the only readily accessible shore. There are many fine beaches around both towns: **Araruna** (2 km from Soure; take supplies and supplement with coconuts and crabs), from where it's a beautiful walk along the shore to **Praia do Pesqueiro**, a magnificent beach 13 km from Soure; (bus from Praça da Matriz at 1030, returns 1600, or on horseback from the Casarão da Amazônia, food available at maloca); and **Caju-Una** and **Céu** 15 km and 17 km from Soure. These are equally fine beaches: 400-m broad stretches washed by a limpid sea. Both are almost deserted, and at the far end Céu extends north into a seemingly interminable expanse of beach and virgin rainforest which stretches over 100 km north to the gentle mangrove-lined cape where Marajo eventually meets the open (but still sweet ocean).

Praia de Joanes between the point of arrival on Marajó (Porto de Camará) is another popular place to stay. It has a laid-back feel, some impressive Jesuit ruins and cliffs overlooking the beach. In the far south of the Marajó archipelago are the little towns of **Ponta de Pedras**, with a few colonial buildings and a fine beach, and **Breves** in the midst of towering rainforest, which runs northwest to areas inhabited only by indigenous people.

Fishing boats make the eight-hour trip to **Cachoeira do Arari** (one hotel, **D**), where there is a fascinating **Marajó museum**. A 10-hour boat trip from Ponta de Pedras goes to the **Arari Lake** where there are two villages: **Jenipapo** and **Santa Cruz**. The latter is less primitive and less interesting; a hammock and a mosquito net are essential.

Santarém and Eastern Pará → *For listings, see pages 58-70.*

Santarém → *Phone code: 093. Population: 262,500.*

The third largest city on the Brazilian Amazon is small enough to walk around in a morning. It was founded in 1661 as the Jesuit mission of Tapajós; the name was changed to Santarém in 1758. There was once a fort here, and attractive colonial squares overlooking the waterfront still remain. Standing at the confluence of the Rio Tapajós with the Amazon, on the southern bank, Santarém is halfway (three days by boat) between Belém and Manaus. Most visitors breeze in and out of town on a stopover.

Santarém

Where to stay
Brasil **1**
Brasil Grande **2**
Grão Rios **6**
Horizonte **3**
Mirante **4**
New City **5**
Santarém Palace **7**

Restaurants
Mascote **2**
Mascotinho **3**
Piracaia **4**
Sabor Caseiro **5**

Blood crop

Ten years ago Santarém was surrounded by trees. Since then, the ranchers have arrived and the trees are disappearing, just as they are further south in Mato Grosso and the Goiás *cerrado* forests, in order to make way for lucrative soya plantations. In 2003 the huge multinational company Cargill built a soya grain terminal in Santarém so that the crop could be transferred to ocean going vessels in the north of the country and not the south. The decision had a far reaching impact. The road cutting up to Santarém from the centre west was renovated and agriculture began to expand into the Amazon. With such an easy means of export on the city's doorstep, developers moved in to Santarém itself, claiming they would bring food and jobs to the poor. The area occupied by farms around the city rose rapidly to over 750 sq km and was planted on land that had been cleared from secondary forest, as well as some 10% on newly felled rainforest Indigenous *caboclo* communities who had made their homes on the land coveted by the farmers were displaced. The ranchers came armed with a ream of false title deeds – just as they did with the *caiçairas* on the Costa Verde. Some *caboclos* sold up. Others were forced off through threats of violence. A few stubbornly stayed. They were intimidated, then beaten. Some were killed. Very few found work on the plantations where the machinery is high tech and the manpower required minimal. And the soya plantations continued to expand.

In 2006 Brazil became the world's biggest soya exporter. After a long Greenpeace campaign, in June 2008 the Brazilian environmental minister Carlos Minc called for a deal to curb appropriation of land for soya farms. But Brazil has a powerful elite and a long history of lip service. The country's current strict environmental legislation is rarely enforced. So for now the vegetarian option is as complicit in death and deforestation as hardwood tables or beef.

Arriving in Santarém **Aeroporto Maestro Wilson Fonseca** ① *15 km from town, Praça Eduardo Gomes, s/n, T093-3523 4328*, receives flights from Fortaleza, Belém, Salvador, Brasília, Manaus and other towns in the Amazon. From the **rodoviária** ① *outskirts of town, T093-3522 3392*, buses run to the waterfront near the market, US$1. Boats from Belém and Manaus dock at the **Cais do Porto**, 1 km west of town (take 'Floresta-Prainha', 'Circular' or 'Circular Externo' bus; taxi US$7); boats from other destinations, including Macapá, dock by the waterfront near the centre of town. The tourist office, **Comtur** ① *R Floriano Peixoto 777, T/F093-3523 2434, Mon-Fri 1000-1700*, has good information available in English. Also see www.paraturismo.pa.gov.br. ▸▸ *See Transport, page 68.*

Places in Santarém In front of the market square, the yellow Amazon water swirls alongside the green blue Tapajós river at the **meeting of the waters**, which is nearly as impressive as that of the Negro and Solimões near Manaus (see page 81). A small **Museu dos Tapajós** ① *Centro Cultural João Fora, on the waterfront, downriver from where the boats dock*, has a collection of ancient Tapajós ceramics, as well as various 19th-century artefacts. The unloading of the fish catch between 0500 and 0700 on the waterfront is interesting.

There are good beaches nearby on the Rio Tapajós. Prainha, a small beach, is between town and the port, by a park with many mango trees (Floresta–Prainha bus from centre). On the outskirts of town is Maracanã, with sandy bays (when the Tapajós is low) and some trees for shade (Maracanã bus from the centre, 20 minutes). Santarém has been at the centre of rapid deforestation in the last decade – fuelled by soya (see box opposite).

Alter do Chão

Alter do Chão (http://alterdochao.tur.br) is a friendly village sitting next to a brilliant white spit of talcum-powder fine sand (known cheesily as Love Island to locals) which juts into the deep blue Rio Tapajós 34 km west of Santarém. It is a very popular beach destination and has a proliferation of restaurants and *pousadas*. There is kayaking and light ecotours on Lago Verde, a lake lined with white-sand beaches in the dry season next to Alter do Chão village. Increasing numbers of tour operators offer trips into the forest from Alter do Chão rather than Santarem. Every second week of September, and Alter do Chao celebrates one of Para's biggest festivals, the **Festa do Çairé**, which sees big-costumed processions in the sandy streets and a pageant depicting the seduction of a river dolphin by a beautiful *cabocla* (river peasant) girl.

Floresta Nacional do Tapajós

ⓘ *Information from Paratur in Belém, www.paraturismo.pa.gov.br.*

This 545,000-ha reserve on the eastern banks of blue Tapajós river, some 120 km south of Santarém, is home to 26 riverine communities who eke a living from harvesting Brazil

Around Santarém

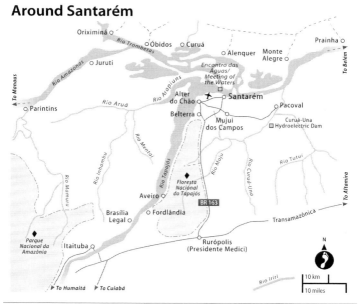

nuts, rubber and from fishing. The protected area forms part of a larger reserve spanning both banks of the river. On the less accessible west shore is the 648,000-ha **Reserva Extrativista Tapajós Arapiuns**, created to allow local people to extract rubber and nuts, hunt on a small scale to reduce environmental impact on the forest. Both areas are open to tourism and agencies in Santarém offer trips which include Amazon homestays with riverine communities. The forests themselves are not as wild as those in similar reserves in Acre but the area is stunningly beautiful, with white-sand beaches, pink river dolphins and the forest itself with its many towering Kapok and Brazil nut trees. ▸▸ *Trips can be organized with tour operators in Santarém, see page 66.*

Belterra and Fordlândia → *Phone code 093.*

Fordlândia, 300 km south of Santarém, was Henry Ford's first rubber plantation. He founded it in 1926 in an attempt to provide a cheaper source of rubber for his Ford Motor Company than the British and Dutch controlled plantations in Malaya. There is **Hotel Zebu**, in old Vila Americana (turn right from the dock, then left up the hill), one restaurant, two bars and three shops on the town square. There is a little pebble beach north of town.

Closer to Santarém, 37 km south on a dirt road, is **Belterra**, where Henry Ford established his second rubber plantation. In the highlands overlooking the Rio Tapajós. It is nearer to the town than his first project, which was turned into a research station. At Belterra, Ford built a well laid-out town, where the houses resemble the cottages of Michigan summer resorts, many with white paint and green trim. The town centre has a large central plaza that includes a bandstand, the church of Santo Antônio (circa 1951), a Baptist church and a large educational and sports complex. A major hospital, which at one time was staffed by physicians from North America, is now closed.

Ford's project, the first modern attempt to invest in the Amazon, was unsuccessful. It was difficult to grow the rubber tree in plantation conditions, where it was unprotected from the heavy rains and harsh sun, and indigenous parasites were attracted by the concentrations of trees. Boats could only come this far upriver in the rainy season and there was a series of disputes between the American bosses and the local employees. Ford sold up in 1945 and the rubber plantation is now deserted.

Alenquer

This tiny town on the opposite bank of the Amazon river to Santarém sits in pretty forest dotted with waterfalls, clear-water streams and strangely eroded tower-like rock formations, the most impressive of which is the Cidade dos Deuses (City of the Gods), some 40 km from town. The easiest way to visit the attractions is either on an organized tour from Santarém or through a *pousada* in Alenquer itself. There are daily boats to Alenquer from the docks in Santarém (speed boats take two to three hours, US$15) or slow boats (US$5, six hours). Boats to and from Belém stop at Alenquer. For more information see www.alenquerpara.com.br.

Monte Alegre

There's not much to this small village, which may have changed ideas about the history of Brazil, and perhaps the Americas (see box opposite) – just a collection of low, scruffy buildings gathered around a street on a shallow hill rising from the vast swampy expanses of the Amazon river. Outside the town, in the municipality of Campina, is the

Monte Alegre

Monte Alegre is the site of archaeological discoveries that have threatened to radically alter current views of the spread of civilization in South America. In the 1990s, Dr Anna C Roosevelt, of the Field Museum of Natural History, Chicago, found pottery fragments in a cave which, according to radiocarbon dating, appear to be from 7000-8000 BC. This pre-dates by some 3000 years what was thought to be the earliest ceramic ware in South America (from Colombia and Ecuador). Subsequent artefacts discovered here, however, have radiocarbon dates of 15,000 BC, which calls for a significant rethink of the original idea that people moved from the Andes into the Amazon Basin. These finds suggest that the story of the people of the Americas is more diverse than hitherto understood.

The cave that Dr Roosevelt excavated is called Caverna da Pedra Pintada. Also in the area are pictographs, with designs of human and animal figures and geometric shapes. Trips can be arranged; many thanks to Philip W Hummer, who sent us a description of a tour led by Dr Anna Roosevelt.

Parque Estadual de Monte Alegre (Monte Alegre State Park) – 5800 ha of lowland forest broken by sedimentary escarpment. This was where Anna Roosevelt made her excavations in the 1990s and is an extraordinary place. The cliffs, crags and caves in the escarpment are covered with hundreds of blood-red paintings. Some show strange figures with pyramidical bodies and bulbous heads surrounded by halos, others symmetrical checker board designs, dancing figures and vibrant hand patterns. Visiting the state park is difficult. Trips can be organized through *pousadas* in town, or with advance notice through Gil Serique (see page 66) in Santarém. For more information see www.montealegre.rec.br.

Óbidos → *Phone code: 093. Population: 46,500.*

Óbidos is the last major town between Santarém and the border with Amazonas state. It is located at the narrowest and deepest point on the river where, millions of years ago, the Amazon (which at that stage was a giant lake in the middle of Brazil) squeezed through the gap in the Guyana and Brazilian highlands to meet the Atlantic. The town was strategically important in the Portuguese expansion of the Amazon. The **Forte Pauxi** (Praça Coracy Nunes, 1697) is a reminder of this fact. Today, Óbidos is a picturesque and clean city with many beautiful tiled buildings and some pleasant parks. Worth seeing are the **Prefeitura Municipal** ⓘ *T093-3547 1194*, the *cuartel* and the **Museu Integrado de Óbidos** ⓘ *R Justo Chermont 607, Mon-Fri 0700-1100 and 1330-1730*. There is also a **Museu Contextual**, which consists of a system of plaques with detailed explanations of historic buildings throughout town. Boating and fishing trips can be arranged and there is a popular beach at **Igarapé de Curuçambá** (with bus connections).

The small airport has flights to Manaus, Santarém and Parintins. Óbidos is five hours upriver from Santarém by boat (110 km). A poor road runs east to Alenquer, Monte Alegre and Prainha and west to Oriximiná, impassable in the wet season.

Amapá and Pará listings

For hotel and restaurant price codes and other relevant information, see pages 10-13.

Where to stay

Macapá *p41, map p41*

$$$ Atalanta, Av Coracy Nunes 1148, T096-3223 1612, www.atalantahotel.com.br. By far the best hotel in town with a rooftop pool and comfortable modern a/c rooms with bathrooms. Includes a generous breakfast. 10 mins' walk from the river.

$$$ Ceta Ecotel, R do Matodouro 640, Fazendinha, T096-3227 3396, www.ecotel.com.br. A rainforest-themed hotel with sloths and monkeys in the trees and a series of trails. All the furniture is made on site. 20 mins from the town by taxi.

$$$ Macapá, Av Francisco Azarias Neto 17, on the waterfront, T096-3217 1350, ww.macapahotel.com.br. The city's grandest hotel, overlooking the river, with a pool, tennis courts and children's play area. Rooms are past their best. Popular with families from Guyane.

$$$-$$ Pousada Ekinox, R Jovino Dinoá 1693, T096-3223 0086, www.ekinox.com.br. One of the best in town, with chalets set in a little tropical garden and with a library. Helpful, French-speaking staff and a good restaurant.

$$ Frota Palace, R Tiradentes 1104, T096- 2101 3999, www.hotelfrota.com.br. Plain, faded rooms with en suites. Airport pickup US$7.

$$ Gloria, Leopoldo Machado 2085, T096-3222 0984. A clean, well-kept, simple hotel with a/c rooms all with en suite, TV and hot water. Breakfast included in the price.

$ Mercúrio, R Cândido Mendes 1300, 2nd floor, T096-3224 2766. Very basic, but close to Praça São José (where the bus from Porto Santana stops).

$ Holliday, Av Henrique Gallúcio 1623, T096-3223 3122. Very simple, though recently repainted, little boxy a/c rooms 20 mins' walk from the river. Breakfast included.

$ Santo Antônio, Av Coriolano Jucá 485, T096-3222 0226. Very simple and slightly musty downstairs rooms and brighter a/c rooms upstairs.

$ Vista Amazônica, Av Beira Rio 1298 (about 1.5 km beyond the Cantino Baiano restaurant away from town), T096-3222 6851. A simple *pousada* and restaurant sitting right opposite the Amazon, with simple but well-maintained tiled rooms with en suites.

Oiapoque *p43*

There are plenty of cheap hotels in Oiapoque, but they are not well maintained. The noisiest and least reputable are closest to the river; the best a few blocks behind.

Belém *p43, maps p45 and p46*

A series of new openings and renovations has seen Belém's hotels improve greatly, although they are still not up to much. All are fully booked during **Círio** (see page 64). There are many cheap hotels close to the waterfront (none too safe) and several others near the *rodoviária* (generally OK).

$$$ Itaoca Belém, Av Pres Vargas 132, T091-4009 2400, www.hotelitaoca.com.br. Well-kept, bright, no-nonsense a/c rooms with writing desks and en suites. The best are on the upper floors away from the street noise, and with river views. Decent breakfast.

$$$ Machado's Plaza, R Henrique Gurjão 200, T091-4008 9800, www.machadosplaza hotel.com.br. Bright, brand-new boutique hotel with smart and tastefully decorated a/c rooms, a small business centre, plunge pool and a pleasant a/c breakfast area. Good value.

$$$ Regente, Av Gov José Malcher 485, T091-3181 5000, www.hregente.com.br. Small, newly refurbished a/c rooms decorated in cream and white tile and with standard 3-star fittings, above a noisy street. Popular with US tour groups.

$$ Le Massília, R Henrique Gurjão 236, T091-3224 2834, www.massilia.com.br. An intimate, French-owned boutique hotel with chic little duplexes and more ordinary doubles. Excellent French restaurant and a tasty French breakfast.

$$-$ Grão Pará, Av Pres Vargas 718, T091-3321 2121, www.hotelgraopara.com.br. Well-kept, new a/c rooms with contemporary fittings and smart en suites in black marble, and a boiler for hot water. The best have superb river views. Excellent breakfast. Great value.

$ Amazônia Hostel, Av Governador Jose Malcher 592, T091-4141 8833, www.amazoniahostel.com.br. It's necessary to make a reservation at this popular hostel. Rooms are a cut above the other very cheap hotels dotted around the decrepit and dank Trav Frutuoso Guimarães and they are situated in a brightly painted rubber boom mansion in a salubrious part of town. Dorms and doubles are very simple; there's no a/c so they can be hot when the windows are closed, and popular with mosquitoes when they aren't. Staff are helpful and some speak English, there's a book exchange, kitchen and breakfast.

$ Novo Avenida, Av Pres Vargas 404, T091-3223 8893, www.hotelnovoavenida.com.br. Slightly frayed but spruce en suite rooms. Decent breakfast. Groups can sleep in cheaper large rooms. Good value.

$ Unidos, Ó de Almeida 545, T091-3224 0660. Simple but spruce, spacious a/c rooms with cable TV and clean en suites. There are other cheap hotels a few doors away if this one is full.

Salinópolis *p50*

$$$ Atalaia, Ilha Atalaia, 15 km from Salinópolis, T/F091-3464 1122. A simple *pousada* in a pleasant setting. Reserve in advance for the weekend, take a taxi.

$$$ Joana d'Arc, Av João Pessoa 555, T/F091-3823 1422. Modest but well looked after and with a generous breakfast.

$$$ Solar, Av Beira Mar, T091-3823 1823. The best in town with smart en suite rooms and a good restaurant.

$$ Diolindina, Av Pres Médici 424, Capanema, T091-821 1667. Small clean a/c rooms with fridge and bath. The price includes breakfast and safe parking. Recommended. There are good restaurants and a supermarket opposite.

Islands around Belém *p50*

Cotijuba

$$-$ Pousada Farol, T091-3259 7144, T091-9943 0237 (mob). Chalets and rooms in annexes set in a little garden right in front of the beach. Good rates during the week. Friendly owners. On the opposite side of the island from the port.

Mosqueiro

There are plenty of opportunities for camping on Mosqueiro and a wealth of *pousadas* in all price brackets.

$$ Farol, Praia Farol, Olha do Mosqueiro, T091-3771 1219. With 1920s architecture but in good repair, small restaurant, rooms face the beach, good views.

$$ Porto Arthur, Av Beira Mar, Praia do Porto Arthur, T091-8145 1438, bookable through www.paratur.com.br. Concrete chalets with verandas, and plain though clean a/c rooms with fridges. These sit over a pool and patio less than 2 mins' walk from the beach. The hotel has a BBQ restaurant, a sauna and paddling pool for kids.

Ilha de Maiandeua and Vila do Algodoal

$$ Jardim do Éden, http://onlinehotel.com.br/para/ilha-do-algodoal/jardim-do-eden- pousada/index.htm. A series of bizarre neo-Gothic brick *cabañas* with kitchenettes overlooking the beach on Praia do Farol. Well kept and well run and with more personality than most on the island. Tours available and camping in the grounds (on the beach). Discounts online.

$$ Pousada Bela-Mar, Av Beira Mar, Vila do Algodoal beach, T091-3854 1128, belamarhotel.blogspot.com. A very simple beachside hotel with tiny rooms, set in a garden. Close to the boat jetty.

$$ Pousada Chalés do Atlântico, Vila do Algodoal, T091-3854 1114, www.algodoal.com.br. Recently renovated. 11 simple little *cabañas* with mosquito screening, en suites and cold showers.

Ilha de Marajó

Marajó gets very busy in the Jul holiday season – be sure to reserve ahead at this time.

$$$ Fazenda Araruna, 14 Rua, Trav 18, outside Soure, T091-3741 1474. A pretty bungalow set on a vast buffalo farm owned by the charming Dona Amélia Barbosa. Offer horse riding, boat and kayak trips and buffalo rides on the beach. Rooms are rustic but comfortable and the price includes an evening meal.

$$$ Pousada dos Guarãs, Av Beira Mar, Salvaterra, T/F091-3765 1133, www.pousadadosguaras.com.br. Well-equipped little resort hotel on the beach with an extensive tour programme.

$$$-$ Casarão da Amazonia, 4 Rua 646, Soure, T091-3741 2222, www.amazzonia.info. The only grand rubber boom mansion in Soure was a ruin until Italian Giancarlo lovingly restored it into this fabulous sky-blue belle époque boutique hotel in the new millennium. The building sits in its own tropical garden next to a pool and restaurant (serving crispy Neapolitan pizzas). Rooms are comfortable, well-appointed and cool and Giancarlo offers wonderful horseback and boat tours around Marajo. Come for several days.

$$ Canto do Frances, 6 Rua, Trav 8, Soure, T091-3741 1298, www.ocantodofrances. blogspot.com. This French/Brazilian-owned *pousada* 20 mins' walk from the centre offers well-kept, whitewash and wooden-walled rooms in a pretty bungalow sitting in a garden filled with flowers and fruit trees. Breakfast is generous and the owners organize horse riding, canoe and bike trips around Soure. Book ahead to be met at the ferry port.

$$ Paracuary, Rio Paracuary, Soure, T091-3225 5915, www.paracauary.com.br. A/c rooms with en suites in mock colonial chalets around a pool 3 km from Soure and on the banks of the Rio Paracuary.

$$ Ventania, Praia de Joanes, T091-3646 2067, www.pousadaventania.com. Pretty little cliff-top *pousada* in a lawned garden a stroll from the beach. Each apartment has room for 2 couples **$**. Bike rental, French, Dutch, English and Spanish spoken.

$ Araruna, Rua 7, Trav 14, Soure. Very simple fan-cooled rooms some of which are decidedly musty (look at a few), but this is the best cheapie in town.

Santarém *p53, map p53*

All hotels, except **Amazon Park**, are in the compact grid of streets in the heart of the city near the waterfront.

$$$ Amazon Park, Av Mendonça Furtado 4120, T091-3523 2800, amazon@ stm.inter conect.com.br. Large 1970s hotel, 4 km from the centre, with a pool and friendly staff.

$$ Brasil Grande Hotel, Trav 15 de Agosto 213, T091-522 5660. Family-run. Restaurant.

$$ New City, Trav Francisco Corrêa 200, T091-523 3149. Standard town hotel with plain a/c rooms and an airport pickup service. River trips can be organized from here.

$$-$ Santarém Palace, Rui Barbosa 726, T091-3523 2820. A 1980s hotel with 44 comfortable but simple a/c rooms with TV and fridge.

$ Brasil, Trav dos Mártires 30, T091-3523 5177. Pleasant, family-run, with fan-cooled rooms with shared bathrooms, breakfast and a small restaurant.

$ Grão Rios, in a little alley off Av Tapajós between Trav dos Mártires and 15 de Agosto. Well-kept a/c rooms, some with a river view.

$ Horizonte, Trav Senador Lemos, 737, T091-3522 5437, horizontehotel@bol.com.br. Plain, simple, well-kept rooms with a/c or fan.
$ Mirante, Trav Francisco Correa 115, T091-3523 3054, freephone T0800-707 3054, www.mirantehotel.com. One of the new and cleaner cheapies. A/c rooms with fridges, TVs, and some with a balcony and individual safes. Internet facilities available. Recommended.

Alter do Chão *p55*
$$ Belas Praias Pousada, R da Praia s/n at the *praça*, T093-3527 1365. Belaspraias@gmail.com. Located on the river front of the beaches, and offering the best rooms – a/c and well appointed with river views.
$$ Agualinda Hotel, R Dr Macedo Costa s/n, T093-3527 1314. A comfortable, clean modern hotel with friendly staff who can help organize forest and river tours.
$ Albergue Pousada da Floresta, T093-3527 1172, www.alberguedafloresta.com. A simple backpacker hostel with basic cabanas and a very cheap open-space for slinging hammocks. Facilities include tour organizing, canoe and bike rental, kitchen and in a great location next to the forest just south of the village. Prices include breakfast. Ask for Angelo.

Belterra *p56*
$ Hotel Seringueira. 8 simple fan-cooled rooms and a pleasant restaurant.

Óbidos *p57*
$$ Braz Bello, R Corrêia Pinto, on top of the hill. Clean rooms with shared bathrooms. Optional full board.
$$-$ Pousada Brasil, R Corrêia Pinto. Basic with fan-cooled rooms with en suites or shared bathrooms.

🍴 Restaurants

Macapá *p41, map p41*
The waterfront *praça* has many open-air restaurants and bars, concentrated at the *trapiche* (pier). These are lively after 1800, especially at weekends.
$$$ Chalé, Av Pres Vargas 499, T096-3222 1970. The best restaurant in the city with good fish, Brazilian dishes and a pleasant atmosphere.
$$ Cantinho Baiano, Av Beira-Rio 1, T096-3223 4153. Overlooking the river 10 mins' walk south of the fort and with some of the best river fish in town. There are many other restaurants along this stretch about 1.5 km beyond the Cantinho Baiano.
$$ Flora, Rodovia Salvador de Diniz 1370-A, Km 15, T096-3283 2858. A lively little restaurant on the riverside next to a little marina 15 km from the fort (travelling away from town). Good fish and local dishes; try the fish infused with energetic Amazon fruits.
$ Bom Paladar Kilo's, Av Pres Vargas 456, T096-223 0555. Pay-by-weight buffet with excellent ice cream made from local fruits; make sure you try the *cupuaçu*.
$ Divina Arte, Av Pres Vargas 969, T096-3222 1877. A decent lunchtime menu restaurant and per kilo buffet. Plenty of choice.
$ Divina Gula, Av Pres Vargas 993, T096-3083 2091. Pleasant little café serving coffee, cakes and snacks.
$ Sarney, R Gal Rondon 1501. Simple but very cheap and filling per kilo restaurant. Good value. Lunchtime only.

Oiapoque *p43*
Gourmets will find themselves in a desert but there are many cheap places serving fish, beans and rice, and several spit-and-sawdust bars in the blocks around the river.

Belém *p43, maps p45 and p46*
All the major hotels have upmarket restaurants. There are numerous outdoor snack bars serving far cheaper meals. Good snack bars serving *vatapá* (Bahian dish) and *tapioca* rolls are concentrated on **Assis de Vasconcelos** on the eastern side of the Praça

da República. There are many decent a/c restaurant, bar and café options in the smart and newly renovated **Estação das Docas** on the riverfront where the boats dock.

$$$ Açaí, Hilton Hotel, Av Pres Vargas 882, T091-3242 6500. Come for lunch or dinner daily, or Sun brunch. Regional dishes such as roasted duck with *tucupi* sauce and jambo leaves.

$$$ Boteco das Onze, Praça FC Brandão s/n, T091-3224 8599. Just about the best regional cooking in Belém with live music every night and a view out over the river. Packed at weekends. Try the *filetena brasa* or the excellent *tambaqui*.

$$$ Churrascaria Rodeio, Rodovia Augusto Montenegro, Km 4, T091-3248 2004. A choice of 20 cuts of meat and 30 buffet dishes for a set price. Well worth the short taxi ride to eat all you can.

$$$ Churrascaria Tucuruvi, Trav Benjamin Constant 1843, Nazaré, T091-3235 0341. Enormous slabs of pork, beef, lamb and a range of sausages; all in vast portions and served with salads and accompaniments.

$$ Cantina Italiana, Trav Benjamin Constant 1401, T091-225 2033. Excellent Italian, with hotel delivery.

$$ Lá em Casa, Estação das Docas. Very good local cooking, especially the buffet and the à la carte *menu paraense*. Try the excellent *tacacá no tucupi* (an acrid soup with prawns cooked with jambo leaves that make the mouth go numb).

$$ Le Massilia, see Where to stay. French-owned and run with dishes including frogs' legs, *sole meunière* and *magret de canard*. Excellent cocktails.

$$ Manjar das Garças, Praça Carniero da Rocha s/n, Arsenal da Marinha, Mangal das Garças, T091-3242 1056. Huge lunch and evening buffet. The restaurant sits next to the river in a small park filled with scarlet ibis on the edge of town. Taxis US$5. Well worth it for an all you can eat meal at weekends.

$$ Sabor Paraense, R Sen Manoel Barata 897, T091-3241 4391. A variety of fish and meat dishes such as crab in coconut milk served in a bright, light dining room.

$$-$ Mãe Natureza, R Manoel Barata 889, T091-3212 8032. Lunch only. Vegetarian and wholefood dishes in a bright clean dining room.

$ Doces Bárbaros, R Benjamin Constant 1658, T091-3224 0576. Lunch only. Cakes, snacks, sandwiches and decent coffee in a/c surrounds.

$ Govinda, R Ó de Almeida 198. Lunch only. Basic but tasty vegetarian food.

$ Portinha, R Dr Malcher 434, T091-3223 0922. Thu-Sun evenings only. Wonderful pastries, *takaka*, *cames* and juices.

Salinópolis *p50*

$ Bife de Ouro, Av Dr Miguel Santa Brígida, opposite petrol station. Simple, but excellent for fish and shrimp. Always busy at lunchtime.

$ Gringo Louco, 15 km (take taxi or hitch), at Cuiarana beach (follow signs). The US owner serves good, unusual dishes, and some 'wild' drinks known as 'bombs'. Popular.

Islands around Belém *p50*

$$ Hotel Ilha Bela, Av 16 de Novembro 409, Mosqueiro. No evening meals. Recommended for fish.

$$ Marésia, Praia Chapeu Virado, Mosqueiro. Highly recommended.

$ Sorveteria Delícia, Av 16 de Novembro, Mosqueiro. Serves good local fruit ice creams and the owner buys dollars.

Ilha de Marajó

There are a number of cheap places to eat in Soure but few restaurants of any distinction.

$ Canecão, Praça da Matriz, Soure. Sandwiches and standard beans, rice and cheap meals. Recommended.

Santarém *p53, map p53*

As with other small towns in the interior of Brazil, most restaurants in Santarém serve basic café-style food, lunch (consisting of rice, beans, chips and a choice of beef, chicken or fish) and juices. The best choice is to be found along the waterfront in the centre.

$$ Mascote, Praça do Pescador 10, T091-3523 2844. Open 1000-2330. Fish-orientated restaurant with a bar and ice cream parlour. Avoid *piraracu*.

$$ Mascotinho, Praça Manoel de Jesus Moraes, on the riverfront. Bar and pizzeria attracting a lively crowd at sunset. Great river view.

$$ Santo Antônio, Av Tapajós 2061, T091-3523 2356. Barbecued meat and fish.

$ Piracaia, R Floriano Peixoto 557, Centro, T091-3522 2881. The best value quality per kilo restaurant in town with a great choice of meat, fish and a few veggie options. General Brazilian cuisine.

$ Sabor Caseiro, R Floriano Peixoto 521, Centro, T091-3522 5111. Northern cooking with Takaka soups, river fish and prawn dishes alongside the usual chicken/meat and rice, beans and chips.

Alter do Chão *p55*

$ Lago Verde, Praça 7 de Setembro. Good fresh fish, try *calderada de tucunaré*.

Óbidos *p57*

There are plenty of cheap fish restaurants near the waterfront and in the upper town.

🎵 Bars and clubs

Macapá *p41, map p41*
The food and drink kiosks in **Complexo Beira Rio** have live music most evenings. **ETNA** is the current dance club of choice, vibrating to the frenetic local rhythm *brega*, which sounds like *forró* on speed.

Belém *p43, maps p45 and p46*
Belém has some of the best and most distinctive live music and nightlife in northern Brazil. It's well worth heading out on the town at weekends.

A Pororó, Av Senador Lemos 3316, Sacramenta, T091-3233 7631. Bands like Calypso made their names in these vast, steaming warehouse clubs. Every Fri and Sat they are packed to the girders with scantily-clad blue-collar locals dancing wildly to techno *brega* acts – usually comprising a platinum blonde with a tiny skirt and Amazonian thighs backed by a band and a troupe of male dancers. A few hours here may be as cheesy as it comes but they are immense fun and barely known even to Brazilian tourists.

Baía Cool Jazz Club, Av Almirante Tamandaré 1, between R do Arsenal and R de Breves, T091-3289 6632. The jazz café of Belém, with national and international acts and local bands of all kinds – from rock, carimbó-fusion, reggae and jazz. Shows are followed by DJs who play underground sounds in the dark cellar bar.

Bar do Gilson, Trav Padre Eutíquio 3172, T091-3272 1306. A covered courtyard space decorated with arty black and white photography and with live Rio de Janeiro *samba* and *choro* on weekends. The bar owner, Gilson often plays mandolin in the band.

Boteco das Onze, Praça Frei Caetano Brandão s/n, Complexo Feliz Lusitânia, T091-3224 8599. This restored colonial fort and mansion is a favourite haunt for Belém's 20- and 30-something upper-middle classes who gather to sip cold draught beer on the veranda or dance inside to live Belém MPB. Wonderful views out over the river and decent food.

Café Com Arte, Av Rui Barbosa 1436 (between Braz de Aguiar and Nazaré), Nazaré, T091-3224 8630. A brightly painted colonial house turned bar and club and with 3 floors devoted to live Belém rock, MPB fusion and DJs – some of whom play avante garde techno *brega*. Attracts an alternative studenty crowd and is especially busy on Fri. At its best after 2300.

Carrousel, Av Almirante Barroso at Antônio Baena. Up-tempo techno-*brega* with twanging guitars, played by DJs on a sound stage that looks like the flight control gallery for a 1970s starship. The club is invariably jam-packed with revellers and the atmosphere and spectacle have to be experienced. Every Fri.

Ibiza, R Jerônimo Pimentel 201, between Av Visconde de Souza Franco and Av Almirante Wandenkolk, Umarizal; T091-3222 0562, www.ibizabelem.com.br. Lively club-bar with live rock, funk and MPB and DJs. Very popular but far from cutting edge.

Mormaço, Passagem Carneiro da Rocha s/n, next to Mangal das Garças, T091-3223 9892, www.mormaco.net. A warehouse-sized building on the waterfront which showcases some of the best live bands in Belém at weekends, playing local rhythms like *carimbó* and Brazilianized reggae and rock.

São Mateus, Trav Padre Eutíquio 606, next to the Praça da Bandeira, Campina, T091-3252 5338. Another of Belém's pretty colonial houses turned street bar. Live bands of every kind; including new acts and space for some 300 people sipping ice-cold beer, caipirinhas and munching *comidinha* bar snacks.

Entertainment

Macapá *p41, map p41*
Art galleries Cândido Portinari, corner of R Cândido Mendes and Av Raimundo Álvares da Costa. Exhibitions of local art.

Cinemas In Macapá Shopping, R Leopoldo Machado 2334.

Theatre Teatro das Bacabeiras, R Cândido Mendes. Concerts, poetry and plays.

Belém *p43, maps p45 and p46*
Art galleries Debret, R Arcipreste Manoel Theodoro 630, Batista Campos, T091-222 4046. Contemporary painting and sculpture, also has library specializing in art and philosophy.
Casa das 11 Janelas (1768), Praça Frei Caetano Brandão, T091-3219 1105.

Cultural performances and art exhibitions, panoramic view.

Cinema Olímpia, Av Pres Vargas 918, T091-3223 1882. The 1st cinema in Belém, opened over 80 years ago, but now shows films for lonely men. But **Nazaré** a few doors down is respectable and there are plenty of multiplexes in the city's shopping malls.

Theatre Margarida Schiwwazappa, Av Gentil Bittencourt 650, T091-3222 2923.

Festivals

Macapá *p41, map p41*
Apr/May Marabaixo is the traditional music and dance festival held for 40 days after Easter.
Jun The Sambódromo has parades of Escolas de Samba at **Carnaval** and **Quadrilhas** during **São João**.
14 Aug Festa de São Joaquim in Curiaú.

Belém *p43, maps p45 and p46*
Apr Maundy Thu, half-day; Good Fri, all shops closed, all churches open and there are processions.
9 Jun Corpus Christi.
15 Aug Accession of Pará to Independent Brazil.
7 Sep Independence Day, commemorated on the day with a military parade, and with a student parade on the preceding Sun.
Sep Festa do Çairé, Santarém and Alter do Chão. Parades in the streets in Alter do Chão with 2 teams competing to out-dance and out-costume each other – the Boto Cor do Rosa (pink river dolphin) and the Boto Tucuxi (gray river dolphin) teams.
30 Oct Círio. The festival of candles, based on the legend of Nossa Senhora de Nazaré whose image was found on the site of her Basílica around 1700. On the 2nd Sun in Oct a procession carries the Virgin's image from the Basílica to the cathedral; it is returned 2 weeks later. The festival attracts many artists

and musicians and has become a massive national celebration with carnival performers and rock groups. Highly recommended. See www.ciriodenazare.com.br
2 Nov All Souls' Day.
8 Dec Immaculate Conception.
24 Dec Christmas Eve, half-day.

Santarém *p53, map p53*
22 Jun Foundation of the city.
29 Jun São Pedro, with processions of boats on the river and Boi-Bumba dance dramas.
8 Dec Nossa Senhora da Conceição, the city's patron saint.

Alter do Chão *p55*
2nd week in Sep Festa do Çairé, religious processions and folkloric events. Recommended.

○ Shopping

Macapá *p41, map p41*
Macapá and Porto Santana were declared a customs-free zone in 1992. There are now many cheap imported goods available from shops in the centre. In the handicraft complex **Casa do Artesão**, Av Azárias Neto, Mon-Sat 0800-1900, craftsmen produce their wares on site. A feature is pottery decorated with local manganese ore, also woodcarvings and leatherwork.

Belém *p43, maps p45 and p46*
There is an arts and crafts market in the **Praça da República** every weekend selling attractive seed and bead jewellery, wicker, hammocks and raw cotton weave work, toys and other knick-knacks. Belém is a good place to buy hammocks: look in the street parallel to the river, 1 block inland from **Ver-o-Peso**. There is a bookshop with English titles in the arcade on **Av Pres Vargas**.
Complexo São Brás, Praça Lauro Sodré. Has a handicraft market and folkloric shows in a building dating from 1911.

Ná Figueredo, Av Gentil Binttencourt 449, Nazaré and Estação das Docas, T091-3224 8948, www.nafigueredo.com.br. One of the best music shops in the north of Brazil selling a wealth of local sounds from the very best bands and unusual music from throughout Brazil. Funky T-shirts and casualwear.
Parfumaria Orion, Trav Frutuoso Guimarães 268. Has a wide variety of perfumes and essences from Amazonian plants, much cheaper than tourist shops.
Shopping Iguatemi, Trav Padre Eutique 1078. Belém's shopping mall.

Islands around Belém *p50*

Ilha de Marajó
Carlos Amaral, 3 Rua, Trav 20. Beautiful Marajo ceramics, made using the same techniques and materials as the Marajoara use themselves. Pieces include large pots and lovely jewellery – with pendants, bracelets and necklaces.

Santarém *p53, map p53*
Muiraquitã, R Lameira Bittencourt 131. Good for ceramics, woodcarvings and baskets.

▲ What to do

Macapá *p41, map p41*

Tour operators
Amapá Turismo, Hotel Macapá, T096-3223 2667. **Fénix**, R Cândido Mendes 374, T/F096-3223 8200, and R Jovino Dinoá 1489, T096-3223 5353.

Belém *p43, maps p45 and p46*

Tour operators
Amazon Star, R Henrique Gurjão 236, T091-3241 8624, T091-3982 7911 (mob), www.amazonstar.com.br. Offers 3-hr city tours and river tours. The company also books airline tickets and hotel on Marajó.

Santarém *p53, map p53*

Tour operators

Amazon Tours, Trav Turiano Meira 1084, T091-3522 1928, T091-3975 1981 (mob), www.amazonriver.com. Owner Steve Alexander is very friendly and helpful and has lots of tips on what to do, he also organizes excursions for groups to Bosque Santa Lúcia with ecological trails. Recommended.

Gil Serique, 80 R Adriano Pimentel, T093-9973 8951, www.gilserique.com. Enthusiastic, larger-than-life, English-speaking tour guide who visits the creeks, flooded forest, primary forests and savannahs around Santarém, including the Tapajos National Park and Maica wetlands. Good on conservation.

Milly Turismo, R Siqueira Campos 277-A, Centro, T091-3523 5938. millyturismo@bol.com.br. Flights, bus tickets tours and very efficient friendly service.

Santarém Tur, R Adriano Pimental 44, T091- 3522 4847, www.santaremtur.com.br. Branch in **Amazon Park Hotel** (see Where to stay). Friendly, helpful foreign-owned company offering individual and group tours (US$50 per person per day for a group of 5), to Tapajós National Forest, Maiça Lake and Fordlândia. Recommended.

⊘ Transport

Macapá *p41, map p41*

Air

Taxis to the airport cost around US$7. There are flights **Belém**, **Brasília**, **Foz do Iguaçu**, **Rio de Janeiro**, **São Paulo**, **São Luís**, **Fortaleza**, **Marabá** and **Cayenne** (Guyane), amongst others.

　　Airline offices Gol, www.voegol. com.br. **META**, airport, T0300-789 5503, www.voemeta.com. **Puma**, T096-3039 3939, www.pumaair.com.br. **TAM**, airport, T096-4002 5700, www.tam.com.br. **Varig**, R Cândido Mendes 1039, T096-3223 4612, www.varig.com.br.

Boat

Boats leave from Porto Santana, which is linked to Macapá by bus or taxi. To **Belém**, *Atlântica*, fast catamaran 8 hrs, 3 times a week, US$30, reservations at **Martinica**, Jovino Dinoá 2010, T096-2235 777. Slower but slightly cheaper boats are *Bom Jesus*, *Comandante Solon*, *São Francisco de Paulo*, *Silja e Souza* of **Souzamar**, Cláudio Lúcio Monteiro 1375, Porto Santana, T096-3281 1946, car ferry with **Silnave**, T096-3223 4011. Purchase tickets from offices 2 days in advance (**Agencia Sonave**, R São José 2145, T096-3223 9090, sells tickets for all boats). Also smaller boats to **Breves** as well as a regular direct service to **Santarém**).

Bus

Estrela de Ouro, office on the main square in front of the cathedral, leaves daily at 2000; and **Cattani**, office on Nunes between São José and Cándido Mendes, leaves daily at 0630 to **Amapá** (US$20), **Calçoene** (US$25, 7 hrs) and **Oiapoque** (12 hrs in the dry season with several rest stops, 14-24 hrs in rainy season, US$35). The Oiapoque bus does not go into Amapá or Calçoene and it is therefore inconvenient to break the trip at these places.

　　Pickup trucks run daily to various locations throughout Amapá: crowded on narrow benches in the back, or pay more to ride in the cab. Despite posted schedules, they leave when full. To **Oiapoque** at 0800, 10-12 hrs, US$35 cab, US$15 in back, to **Lourenço** at 0900.

Car hire

Localiza, R Independência 30, T096-3223 2799, and airport T096-3224 2336. **Sila Rent a Car**, Av Procópio Rola 1346, T096-3224 1443.

Train

Limited services between **Porto Santana** and **Serra do Navio**.

Oiapoque *p43*

Air
Flights to **Macapá** 3 times a week.

Boat
Frequent launches across the river to **Guyane** (US$5, 10 mins). Occasional cargo vessels to **Belém** or **Macapá** (Porto Santana).

Bus
Estrela de Ouro leaves for **Macapá** from the waterfront, twice daily at 1000 and after lunch, 10-12 hrs (dry season), 14-24 hrs (wet season), US$35, also **Cattani**. Pickup trucks depart from the same area when full, US$35 in cab, US$15 in the back. *Combis* to **Cayenne** leave from St-Georges Oyapock in the morning.

Belém *p43, maps p45 and p46*

Air
To get to the airport, take bus 'Perpétuo Socorro-Telégrafo' or 'Icaraci', every 15 mins, from the prefeitura, Praça Felipe Patroni (US$1.50, 40 mins). A taxi to the airport costs US$15. There are flights to most state capitals and many others. Internationally, there are flights to **Cayenne** (Guyane), **Fort-de-France** (Martinique), **Port au Prince** (Haiti), **Paramaribo** (Suriname) and **Miami** (USA).

 Airlines **Air Caribe**, www.caribbean-airlines.com; **GOL**, www.voegol.com.br; **META**, www.voemeta.come; **SETE**, www.voe sete.com.br; **TAM**, www.tam.com.br. **TOTAL**, www.total.com.br.

Boat
Boats leave from the Companhia das Docas at the Armazém 10 dock in town to Porto de Camará near Salvaterra on **Ilha de Marajó**, Mon-Sat 0630 and 1430, Sun 1000. Boats to Marajó also run from the port at Icoaraci (20 km north of Belém, 30 mins by bus from the *rodoviária* or from the Ver o Peso market, taxi

US$25), Mon-Fri 0630, 0730, Sat 1600, 1700, Sun 1600, 1700 and 1800.

There are river services to **Santarém**, **Manaus** (see Routes in Amazônia, page 97) and intermediate ports. The larger ships berth at **Portobrás/Docas do Pará** (the main commercial port), either at Armazém (warehouse) No 3 at the foot of Av Pres Vargas, or at Armazém No 10, a few blocks further north (entrance on Av Marechal Hermes, corner of Av Visconde de Souza Franco). The guards will sometimes ask to see your ticket before letting you into the port area, but tell them you are going to speak with a ship's captain. Ignore the touts who approach you. Smaller vessels (sometimes cheaper, usually not as clean, comfortable or safe) sail from small docks along the **Estrada Nova** (not a safe part of town). Take a **Cremação** bus from Ver-o-Peso.

There is a daily service to **Macapá** (Porto Santana) with *Silja e Souza* of **Souzamar**, Trav Dom Romualdo Seixas, corner of R Jerônimo Pimentel, T091-222 0719, and Comandante Solon of **Sanave** (**Serviço Amapaense de Navegação**, Av Castilho Franca 234, opposite Ver-o-Peso, T091-3222 7810). To **Breves**, ENAL, T091-3224 5210. There are 2 desks selling tickets for private boats in the *rodoviária*; some hotels (eg **Fortaleza**) recommend agents for tickets. Purchase tickets from offices 2 days in advance. Smaller boats to Macapá also sail from Estrada Nova.

Bus
To get to the *rodoviária* take **Aeroclube**, Cidade Novo, No 20 bus, or **Arsenal** or **Canudos** buses, US$0.50, or taxi, US$5 (day), US$7 (night).

Regular bus services to all major cities: **Transbrasiliana** go direct to **Marabá**, US$20 (16 hrs). To **Santarém**, via Marabá once a week (US$45, more expensive than by boat and can take longer, goes only in dry season). To **São Luís**, 2 a day, US$20, 13 hrs,

interesting journey through marshlands.
To **Fortaleza**, US$35-40 (24 hrs), several
companies. To **Salvador**, US$50.
Car hire Avis, R Antônio Barreto 1653, T091-
3230 2000, www.avis.com, also at airport,
T0800- 558 066. **Localiza**, Av Pedro Álvares
Cabral 200, T091-3212 2700, www.localiza.
com.br, and at airport, T091-3257 1541.

Islands around Belém *p50*

Ilha do Marajó

Air
There is a taxi-plane service between Soure
Belém. There are regular flights at weekends
and its is worth ringing ahead to see if there
is any space on a plane.
 Airline offices Aeroval Táxi Aéreo, Av
Senador Lemos (Aeroclube do Pará), T091-
3233 3528; **Táxi Aéreo Soure**, Av Senador
Lemos, Pass São Luiz s/n (Aeroclube do
Pará), T091-3233 4986; **Táxi Aéreo Cândido**,
Av Senador Lemos, Pass São Luiz s/n
(Aeroclube do Pará), T091-9608 9019.

Boat
Boats run from Porto de Camará near
Salvaterra to **Porto de Icoaraci** (Mon-Fri
1600 and 1700, Sat 1600 and 1700, Sun 1600,
1700 and 1800. **Henvil** sell tickets through
their booth at the *rodoviária* (T091-3246
7472). Boats also run from Camará do Porto
to the Armazém 10 dock in **Belém**, Mon-Sat
0630, 1500, Sun 1500 (3 hrs, US$5).
Timetables regularly change so check
beforehand.
 Boat companies Araparí Navegação, R
Siqueira Mendes 120, Cidade Velha, Belém,
T091-3242 1870 and **Companhia Docas do
Pará**, portão 15, T091-3242 1570. **Henvil
Navegação**, Av Bernardo Sayão 4440, Praça
Princesa Isabel, Jurunas, Belém, T091-3249
3400/3246 7472 and **Porto de Icoaraci**, R
Siqueira Mendes s/n.

Santarém *p53, map p53*

Air
The bus to the airport from the centre leaves
from Rui Barbosa every 80 mins, 0550-1910;
taxis US$8. The hotels **Amazon Park**, **New
City** and **Rio Dourado** have free buses for
guests; you may be able to take these. There
are flights to **Belém**, **Fortaleza**, **Manaus**,
Recife, **Salvador**, **São Luís**; **Altamira**,
Itaituba, **Monte Dourado**, **Oriximiná**,
Manaus; **Araguaína**, **Belo Horizonte**,
Brasília, **Carajás**, **Parintins**, **Trombetas**,
Tucuruí, **Uberaba** and **Uberlândia**.
 Airline offices GOL, www.voegol.
com.br, **META**, R Siqueira Campos 162,
T091-3522 6222, www.voemeta.com.br.
Penta, Trav 15 de Novembro 183, T091-
3523 2532. **TRIP**, www.voetrip.com.br.
TAM, www.tam.com.br.

Boats
There are local services to **Óbidos** (US$10,
4 hrs), **Oriximiná** (US$12.50), **Alenquer**,
and **Monte Alegre** (US$10, 5-8 hrs). Boats
for **Belém** and **Manaus** leave from the Cais
do Porto, 1 km west of town (take 'Floresta-
Prainha', 'Circular' or 'Circular Externo' bus;
taxi US$4); boats for other destinations,
including **Macapá**, leave from the waterfront near the centre of town. For further
information on services to Manaus, Belém,
Macapá, Itaituba and intermediate ports, see
Routes in Amazônia, page 97.

Bus
To get to the *rodoviária* take the 'Rodagem'
bus from the waterfront near the market,
US$0.50. To **Itaituba**, US$11, 11 hrs, 2 a day.
To **Marabá** on the Rio Tocantins (via
Rurópolis US$7.50, 6 hrs, and **Altamira**
US$23, 28 hrs), 36 hrs (can be up to 6 days),
US$41, with **Transbrasiliana**. Also to
Imperatriz, via Marabá; office on Av Getúlio
Vargas and at the *rodoviária*. Enquire at the
rodoviária for other destinations. Beware of

vehicles that offer a lift, which frequently turn out to be taxis. Road travel during the rainy season is always difficult, often impossible. Buses to **Belterra** leave from Trav Silvino Pinto between Rui Barbosa and São Sebastião, Mon-Sat 1000 and 1230, US$4, about 2 hrs. There is a 1-hr time difference between Santarém and Belterra, so if you take the 1230 bus you'll miss the 1530 return.

Alter do Chão *p614*

Bus

Tickets and information from the bus company kiosk opposite **Pousada Tupaiulândia**. Buses to **Santarém** leave from the bus stop on Av São Sebastião, in front of Colégio Santa Clara, US$1, about 1 hr.

Belterra and Fordlândia *p615*

Bus

Bus from Belterra to **Santarém** to Belterra Mon-Sat 1300 and 1530, US$4, about 2 hrs. There is a 1-hr time difference between Santarém and Belterra.

Boat

Boats that run **Santarém–Itaituba** stop at Fordlândia if you ask (leave Santarém 1800, arrive 0500-0600, US$12 for 1st-class hammock space); ask the captain to stop for you on return journey, about 2300. Or take a tour with a Santarém travel agent.

❶ Directory

Macapá *p41, map p41*
Banks Banco do Brasil, R Independência 250, and **Bradesco**, R Cândido Mendes 1316, have Plus ATMs for VISA withdrawals. For *câmbios* (cash only), **Casa Francesa**, R Independência 232. **Monopólio**, Av Isaac Alcoubre 80. Both US$ and euros can be exchanged here. Best to buy euros in Belém if heading for Guyane as *câmbios* in Macapá

are reluctant to sell them and they are more expensive and hard to obtain at the border. **Embassies and consulates France**, at Pousada Ekinox (see page 58). Visas are not issued for non-Brazilians. **Internet** @llnet in Macapá Shopping and numerous others. **Medical services** Hospital Geral, Av FAB, T096-3212 6127. **Hospital São Camila & São Luiz**, R Marcelo Candia 742, T096-3223 1514. **Post office** Av Corialano Jucá. **Telephone** R São José 2050, open 0730-2200.

Oiapoque *p43*
Banks It is possible to exchange US$ and reais to euros, but dollar rates are low and TCs are not accepted anywhere. **Banco do Brasil**, Av Barão do Rio Branco, 1000-1500, reais to euros and Visa facilities. Visa users can also withdraw reais at **Bradesco**, exchanging these to euros. Gold merchants, such as **Casa Francesa** on the riverfront and a *câmbio* in the market, will sell reais for US$ or euros. Rates are even worse in St Georges. Best to buy euros in Belém, or abroad. **Immigration** Polícia Federal for Brazilian exit stamp is on the road to Calçoene, about 500 m from the river. **Post office** Av Barão do Rio Branco, open 0900-1200, 1400-1700.

Belém *p43, maps p45 and p46*
Banks Banks open 0900-1630, but foreign exchange only until 1300. **Banco do Brasil**, Av Pres Vargas, near Hotel Itaoca, good rates, ATMs; **Bradesco** throughout the city for ATMs. **HSBC**, Av Pres Vargas near Praça da República has MasterCard Cirrus and Amex ATMs. **Embassies and consulates Suriname**, R Gaspar Viana 488, T091-3212 7144. For visas allow 4 days. **Colombia**, Av Almirante Barroso, 71, apt 601, bloco B, Ed. Narciso Braga, T091-3246 5662. **Venezuela**, R Presidente Pernambuco 270, T091-3222 6396, convenbelem@canal13.com.br. Allow at least 1 day for visas. **UK**, Av Governador José Malcher, 815 – SL 410, T091-3222 0762;

USA, www.embaixada.americana.org.br.
Internet Throughout the city including:
Amazon, 2nd floor of Estação das Docas;
Convert, Shopping Iguatemi, 3rd floor,
US$1.40 per hr; **InterBelém**, Av Jose Malcher
189, US$1 per hr, helpful South African
owner, English spoken. **Language schools**
Unipop, Av Sen Lemos 557, T091-3224 9074,
Portuguese course for foreigners. **Laundry**
Lav e Lev, R Dr Moraes 576. **Lavanderia**
Paraense, Trav Dom Pedro 1104, T091-3222
0057, dry and steam cleaning. **Libraries**
UFPA, Av Augusto Correa 1, T091-3211 1140,
university library with many titles on
Amazônia. **Medical services** A yellow fever
certificate of inoculation is mandatory (see
Health, page 16) It is best to get one at home
(always have your certificate handy).
Medications for malaria prophylaxis are not
sold in Belém pharmacies. You can
theoretically get them through the public
health service, but this is hopelessly
complicated. Such drugs are sometimes
available at pharmacies in smaller centres, eg
Santarém and Macapá. Bring an adequate
supply from home. **Clínica de Medicina**
Preventiva, Av Bras de Aguiar 410
(T091-3222 1434), will give injections,
English spoken, open 0730-1200, 1430-1900
(Sat 0800-1100). **Hospital da Ordem**
Terceira, Trav Frei Gil de Vila Nova 59,
T091-3212 2777, doctors speak some English,
free consultation. Surgery Mon 1300-1900,
Tue-Thu 0700-1100, 24 hrs for emergencies.
The British consul has a list of English-
speaking doctors. **Police** For reporting
crimes, R Santo Antônio and Trav Frei Gil de
Vila Nova. **Post office** Av Pres Vargas 498.
Also handles telegrams and fax.
Telephone Telemar, Av Pres Vargas.

Santarém p53, map p53
Banks There are **Bradescos** in town with
Visa ATMs. **Internet** **Amazon's Star Cyber**,
Av Tapajos, 418 em frente a Orla, T093-3522
3648. Fast connection. English speaking.
Tips and information available. **Global**
Cyber, R Siqueira Campos 175 B, Centro.
Hip grunge/graffiti decor, fast connection,
good a/c, drinks, friendly staff. **Laundry**
Storil, Trav Turiano Meira 167, 1st floor. **Post**
office Praça da Bandeira 81. **Medical**
services Hospital São Raimundo Nonato,
Av Mendonça Furtado 1993, T091-3523 1176.
Telephone **Posto Trin**, R Siqueira Campos
511. Mon-Sat 0700-1900, Sun 0700-2100.

Amazonas and the Amazon River

Amazonas is the largest state in Brazil (1.6 million sq km), bigger than any country in South America except Argentina, but with a population of just 2.8 million. Half of the inhabitants live in the capital, Manaus, with the rest spread out in remote communities often linked only by air and river.

The scenery in Amazonas is magnificent. Nothing can prepare you for the vast skies, the pure air, the endless shades of green, and rivers that stretch to the horizon. Nowhere does the Amazon feel more like the inland sea it once was than here. Rivers merge in vast swirls of myriad shades, from the translucent black of strong iced tea to café-au-lait brown, through vast forest-fringed lakes covered with giant water lilies or through eerie strands of flooded igapó or varzea forest. And in the rivers' depths swim 4-m-long horny-tongued fish, bull sharks, dolphins, stingrays and catfish big enough to swallow a man whole.

Amazonas state preserves Brazil's most extensive and unspoilt areas of lowland tropical forest, and the tourist industry here is developing fast. Most tours and trips to jungle lodges begin in Manaus, a sprawling rubber-boom town with good national and international connections. Beyond Manaus are the giant boulder mountains of the upper Rio Negro, which rise to Brazil's highest peak, the flooded wilds of Mamiraúá Ecological Reserve near Tefé, and the Javari near Tabatinga, which are among the best places in the Amazon for spotting wildlife.

But the vast forests of Amazonas are not uninhabited. Civilizations have been living here from anywhere between 11,000 and 5000 BC and these people and their caboclo descendants maintain a rich cultural life. Although indigenous villages are very difficult to visit, their heritage can be experienced at the festivals in São Gabriel and the Boi Bumba in Parintins. The latter is the largest and most spectacular in the country after Carnaval and takes place on an island in the middle of the Amazon river at the end of June.

Visiting the forest

What to visit

The scenery is at its best on the **Rio Negro**, especially around the **Anavilhanas** archipelago, and further upstream where the mountains of the Guiana Shield punctuate the forest like giant worn crocodile teeth. However, the Rio Negro is an acidic, black-water river and consequently has a lower level of biodiversity than the more PH-neutral brown-water rivers like the Solimões (Amazon). So if you are intent on seeing wildlife, you will see far more in the regions south of Manaus, on the smaller river tributaries, creeks (*igarapés*) and flooded forest areas (*varzea* and *igapós*), especially those that are farthest from people. The **Lago Mamori**, **Lago Piranha** and the **Rio Urubu** are popular destinations for operators in Manaus. These are semi-protected areas which mix wild forests, rivers, creeks, igapo lakes and riverine communities living within nature at minimum impact. Only the farther reaches of either have prolific wildlife, but all offer a taste of the forest, and there are fascinating community tourism projects at Mamori (see **Amazon Gero Tours**, page 95). The best area for wildlife and genuine, accessible wilderness is the **Mamirauá Ecological Reserve** near Tefé, 30-40 minutes by plane from Manaus or 11-12 hours by fast boat. Some of the lodges very close to Manaus have their own reserves, which have been populated with rescued primates and birds. The best of these is **Amazon Ecopark** (see page 90). There are other jungle lodges in Acre and Mato Grosso that are good for wildlife.

When to visit

There is no best time to visit the forest; it depends what you want to see. The Amazon around Manaus is far more than a big river; think of it rather as an inland sea. Water is everywhere, especially during the **wet season**, which lasts from November to May. During the floods, the water rises by 5-10 m and the forests around the main rivers form areas known as *varzea* (on brown-water rivers) and *igapós* (on black-water rivers). Trees are submerged almost to their canopies and it is possible to canoe between their trunks in search of wildlife. In the morning you can often hear the booming call of huge black caiman and the snort of dolphins. And as the boats pass through the trees, startled hatchet fish jump into the bows. It is possible to canoe for tens of kilometres away from the main river flow, as *varzea* and *igapós* often connect one river to another, often via oxbow lakes covered in giant lilies. The lakes are formed when a meandering river changes course and leaves part of its previous flow cut off from the stream. In the **dry season** the rivers retreat into their main flow, exposing broad mudflats (on the brown-water rivers) or long beaches of fine white sand. Caiman and giant river turtles can often be seen basking on these in the evening sun, and wildlife spotting is generally a little easier at this time of year. Trees in the Amazon bear fruit at different times throughout the year; whenever a particular tree is in fruit it attracts large parrots, macaws and primates.

Choosing a tour or lodge

Once you have decided on when and where to go, the next decision is to choose a lodge or an operator. Those used to the quality of wildlife information supplied by rainforest

Coletivo Radio Cipo recommend

Coletivo Radio Cipo, www.myspace.com/coletivoradiocipo, play a vibrant mix of reggae, *carimbó*, roots and rock. They are one of the most exciting bands on the vibrant Belém music scene and often play life in the city. Their singer Carlinhos recommends the following: 'For me the **Bar do Gilson** (see page 63) is a great spot to listen to music, eat and chat. In the 1970s when a group of friends who loved *chorinho* and other such music found there was nowhere to play it in Belém they began to gather here. Some great names have played at the venue over the years, when they pass through Belém, such as Paulino da Viola, Beth Carvalho, Cristina Buarque and Sivuca, together with musicians from Japan, Cuba and other countries. It's a great place and there's always a good show.'

tour operators in Costa Rica, Peru, Ecuador or Bolivia will be disappointed by the lack of professional wildlife knowledge and ecotourism services offered by many of the operators in Manaus. If you are interested first and foremost in wildlife and want accurate information, be sure to request a specialist wildlife guide (see page 96) and question your tour company carefully to test their knowledge. A good way of doing this is to ask whether they can supply a species list for the area around their lodge or for the forests they visit during their tours. Few can. Serious wildlife enthusiasts and birders looking to visit the Brazilian Amazon should think about heading for **Mamirauá Ecological Reserve** near Tefé (see page 84).

That said, the better Manaus tours offer a fascinating glimpse of the forest and filigree of rivers, and insights into river people's lives. And they are far cheaper than Mamirauá. **Standard tours** involve a walk through the forest looking at plants and their usage, caiman spotting at night (many guides drag caiman out of the water, which has negative long-term effects and should be discouraged), piranha fishing and boat trips through the *igapós* (flooded forests) or the *igarapés* (creeks). They may also visit a *caboclo* (river village) or one of the newly established indigenous villages around the city. Other trips involve light adventure such as rainforest survival, which involves learning how to find water and food in the forest, and how to make a shelter and string up a hammock for a secure night's sleep.

Trips vary in length. A half-day or a day trip will usually involve a visit to the 'meeting of the waters' and the Lago de Janauri nature reserve, where you are likely to see plenty of birds, some primates and river dolphins. The reserve was set up to receive large numbers of tourists so there are captive parrots on display and numerous tourist shops. Yet ecologists agree that the reserve helps relieve pressure on other parts of the river. Boats for day trippers leave the harbour in Manaus constantly throughout the day, but are best booked at one of the larger operators. Those with more time can take the longer cruises with a company like **Amazon Clipper** (see page 96) or stay in one of the rainforest lodges. To see virgin rainforest, a five-day trip by boat is needed.

Prices vary but usually include lodging, guide, transport, meals (but not drinks) and activities. The recommended companies charge around US$110-125 per person for a day trip, or US$300-350 for three days.

Beware of the touts

There are many hustlers at the airport in Manaus and on the street (particularly around the hotels and bars on Joaquim Nabuco and Miranda Leão), and even at hotel receptions. It is not wise to go on a tour with the first friendly face you meet. All go-betweens earn a commission so recommendations cannot be taken at face value and employing a freelance guide not attached to a company is potentially dangerous as they may not be qualified; check out their credentials. Tourist offices are not allowed by law to recommend guides, but can provide you with a list of legally registered companies. Unfortunately, disreputable companies are rarely dealt with in any satisfactory manner, and most continue to operate. Book direct with the company itself and ask for a detailed, written contract if you have any doubts. Above all avoid the cheapest tours. They are almost invariably the worst. Choosing a once in the lifetime tour on the basis of price alone is as clever as using plastic bags instead of shoes because they're cheaper.

What to take

Leave luggage with your tour operator or hotel in Manaus and only take what is necessary for your trip. Long-sleeved shirts and long trousers made of modern wicking fabrics, walking boots, insect repellent and a hammock and/or mosquito net, if not provided by the local operator, are advisable for treks in the jungle, where insects can be voracious. A hat offers protection from the sun on boat trips. Powerful binoculars are essential for spotting wildlife (at least 7x magnification is recommended, with the ability to focus at between 2.5 m and infinity). Buying bottled water at the local villages is a sure way to help the local economy, but it can be expensive in the lodges and it produces a great deal of waste plastic that is usually just chucked into the river directly or indirectly. Bring iodine, purification tablets or a modern water filter like PUR Scout or Aquapure (best with iodine for Amazon river water).

Ecotourism best practice in Manaus→ See page 89 for a list of recommended lodges.

Most of the lodges around Manaus do not adhere to proper ecotourism practices; this guide lists the exceptions. Good practice includes integration and employment for the local community, education support, recycling and proper rubbish disposal, and trained guides with good wildlife lodges. Ecotourism in Brazil is often a badge for adventure tourism in a natural setting and few operators conform to the best practices of the International Ecotourism Society, www.ecotourism.org. In Manaus, a relatively small number of communities have benefited from a boom which has seen the total number of beds rise from just six in 1979 to more than 1000 today. Only 27% of labour derives from local communities and very few of the lodges are locally owned. We would love to receive feedback about lodges and operators you feel are (or aren't) making a difference.

Manaus → *For listings, see pages 88-100. Phone code: 092. Population: 1.4 million.*

Manaus, the state capital, sits at 32 m above sea level some 1600 km from the Atlantic. The city sprawls over a series of eroded and gently sloping hills divided by numerous creeks, and stands at the junction of the liquorice-black Rio Negro and the toffee-coloured Solimões, whose waters flow side by side in two distinct streams within the same river. The city is the commercial hub for a vast area including parts of Peru, Bolivia and Colombia, and ocean-going container vessels often dock here.

New-found wealth has turned Manaus from tawdry to tourist-friendly in the last 10 years and the city will be one of the host cities for the 2014 World Cup. The **Centro**

Manaus

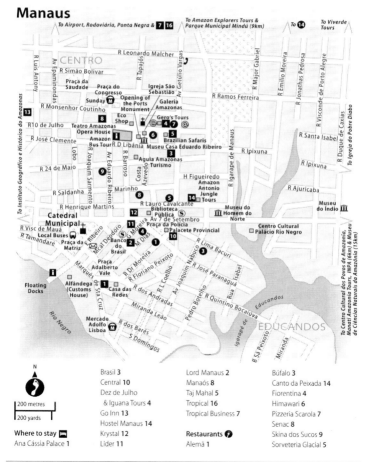

Histórico (old rubber boom city centre), which huddles around the green and gold mock-Byzantine dome of the **Teatro Amazonas** opera house, has been tastefully refurbished and now forms an elegant pedestrian area with cafés, galleries, shops and musuems. The area is a pleasant place to stroll around and sip a cool juice or a strong coffee, and many of the best hotels and guesthouses are found here. There are plenty of restaurants, bars and clubs, which support a lively, colourful nightlife.

Despite the city's size, the forest is ever present on the horizon and always feels just a short boat trip away. Beaches fringe its western extremities at Ponta Negra, whose sands are backed by towering blocks of flats, making it feel like a kind of Amazonian Ipanema.

There are plenty of sights near Manaus. The most vaunted are generally the least interesting. However, the **Anavilhanas** – the largest river archipelago in the world, comprising a beautiful labyrinth of forested islands, some fringed with white-sand beaches lapped by the jet-black waters of the Rio Negro – should not be missed. Try to be there for sunset when thousands of swifts descend to roost and the light is a deep, rich gold.

Manaus is also the main departure point for rainforest tours. There are many lodges around the city, from 20 minutes to four hours away. And although animals here are not as easy to see as in Tefé or on the **Rio Cristalino**, the scenery is breathtaking.

Arriving in Manaus
Air The modern **Eduardo Gomes airport** ① *10 km north of the city centre, T092-3652 1120*, receives flights from all of Brazil's principal cities and there are international connections with Ecuador, Bolivia, Panama and the USA. Airport buses run to the Praça da Matriz restaurant (aka Marques da Santa Cruz), next to the cathedral in the centre of town (every 30 minutes 0500-2300, US$1.50). A taxi to the centre costs around US$29 on the meter. Taxi drivers often tell arrivals that no bus to town is available – be warned.

Road The only usable road runs north to Boa Vista, Guyana and Venezuela (although there are plans afoot to pave the road to Porto Velho for 2014). Visitors almost invariably arrive by plane or boat. The only long-distance buses arriving in Manaus **rodoviária** ① *5 km out of town at the intersection of Av Constantino Nery and R Recife*, are from Boa Vista, Presidente Figueiredo and Itacoatiara. To get to the centre, take a bus marked Praça Matriz or Cidade Nova, US$1.50, taxi US$20.

River Boats run to Santarém, Belém, Parintins, Porto Velho, Tefé, Tabatinga (for Colombia and Peru), São Gabriel da Cachoeira, and intermediate ports. Boat passengers arrive at the newly renovated **floating docks** ① *in the centre, a couple of blocks south of Praça da Matriz*, with direct access to the main artery of Avenida Eduardo Ribeiro, and 10 minutes' walk from the opera house and main hotel area. The docks is open to the public 24 hours a day. Bookings can be made up to two weeks in advance at the ticket sales area by the port's pedestrian entrance, bear left on entry and walk past the cafés. The names and itineraries of departing vessels are displayed here.

Boats for São Gabriel da Cachoeira, Novo Airão, and Caracaraí go from São Raimundo, upriver from the main port. Take bus No 101 'São Raimundo', No 112 'Santo Antônio' or No 110, 40 minutes; there are two docking areas separated by a hill, the São Raimundo *balsa*, where the ferry to Novo Airão, on the Rio Negro, leaves every afternoon (US$10);

and the Porto Beira Mar de São Raimundo, where the São Gabriel da Cachoeira boats dock (most departures are on Friday).

Many boat captains will allow you to sleep on the hammock deck of the boat for a day before departure or after arrival. Be careful of people who wander around boats after they've arrived at a port; they are almost certainly looking for something to steal. Agencies in town can book boat tickets for a small surcharge. ▸▸ *See Transport, page 98.*

Getting around The Centro Histórico and dock areas are easily explored on foot. All city bus routes start on Marquês de Santa Cruz next to the Praça da Matriz and almost all then pass along the Avenida Getúlio Vargas (two blocks east of the Opera House). Taxis can be found near the opera house, at the *rodoviária*, airport and in Ponta Negra. Many of the upmarket hotels are in Ponta Negra, which is 13 km from the city centre and can feel somewhat isolated.

Tourist information There are several **Centros de Atendimento ao Turista (CAT)** ① *main office: 50 m south of the opera house, Av Eduardo Ribeiro 666, T092-3622 0767, Mon-Fri 0800-1700, Sat 0800-1200,* throughout the city. There are also offices in **Amazonas Shopping** ① *Av Djalma Batist 482, Chapada, T096-3236 5154, Mon-Sat 0900-2200, Sun 1500-2100;* at the **airport** ① *T096-3652 1120 or T0800-280 8820, daily 0700-2300;* at the **port** ① *regional terminal, R Marquês de Santa Cruz, armazém 07, Mon-Fri 0800-1700,* and ① *international terminal, R Marquês de Santa Cruz, armazém 10,* which opens only when cruise liners dock. There is a CAT trailer in the **rodoviária** ① *R Recife s/n, Flores, Mon-Sat 0800-1200.*

The **Amazon Bus** ① *T092-2324 5071, www.tucunareturismo.com.br, departures from CAT next to Teatro Amazonas, Mon-Sat 0900 and 1430, US$35, US$17 for children under 12,* is a double decker bus (air-conditioned ground floor and open-top upper deck), which visits the principal attractions in the Manaus on a three-hour, principally drive-by tour with guided commentary in Portuguese. It doesn't represent very good value for time or money. Many of the more interesting sights are not included (notably the Palacete Principal, the floating docks and INPA), there are some bizarre inclusions (like the football stadium, the Olympic village and the Federal University) and there's only one proper stop – at Ponta Negra beach (where the bus breaks for snacks and a breath of warm air).

The website for tourism in the Amazon, www.amazonastur.am.gov.br, has extensive information on accommodation throughout the state in Portuguese and English. *A Crítica* newspaper lists local events.

Centro histórico

The colonial streets that spread out from Teatro Amazonas and Praça São Sebastião are a reminder of Manaus's brief dalliance with wealth and luxury. Eduardo Ribeiro, the state governor who presided over these golden years, was determined to make 19th-century Manaus the envy of the world: a fine European city in which the *nouveau riche* could parade their linen and lace. He spared no expense. Trams were running in Manaus before they were in Manchester or Boston and its roads were lit by the first electric street lights in the world. The city's confidence grew with its majesty. Champagne flowed under the crystal chandeliers and prices rose to four times those of contemporaneous New York. Extravagance begot extravagance and rubber barons eager to compete in statements of affluent vulgarity fed their horses vintage wine or bought lions as guard cats.

In the 1890s, Ribeiro decided to put the icing on his cake, commissioning the Gabinete Português de Engenharia e Arquitetura to build an Italianate opera house, the **Teatro Amazonas** ① *Praça São Sebastião, T096-622 1880, Mon-Sat 0900-1600, 20-min tour US$6, students US$2.50,* and to surround it with stone-cobbled streets lined with elegant houses, plazas, and gardens replete with ornate fountains and gilded cherubs. Masks adorning the theatre walls were made in homage to great European artists, including Shakespeare, Mozart, Verdi and Molière and the driveway was paved in rubber to prevent the sound of carriage wheels spoiling performances. For the lavish interior, Ribeiro turned to the Roman painter **Domenico de Angelis** (who had painted the Opera House in Belém in 1883) and **Giovanni Capranesi** (an Italian colleague who had worked with Angelis on the Igreja de São Sebastião near the Teatro). Their grandiose decorations are magnificent both in their pomp and their execution. They include a series of trompe l'oeuil ceilings – showing the legs of the Eiffel Tower from beneath (in the auditorium) and the muse of the arts ascending to heaven surrounded by putti in the Salão Nobre reception room. Ribeiro also commissioned a Brazilian artist to paint a stage curtain depicting *Iara*, the spirit of the river Amazon at the centre of the meeting of the waters, and a series of scenes of idealized indigenous Brazilian life based on Paulistano Carlos Gomes' opera, *O Guarany*, in the ballrooms. The steel for the building was moulded in Glasgow, the mirrors made in Venice and priceless porcelains from France, China and Japan were purchased to grace mantelpieces, stairwells and alcoves. After the theatre doors were opened in 1896, Caruso sang here and Pavlova danced.

But for all its beauty and expense the theatre was used for little more than a decade. In the early 20th century the rubber economy collapsed. Seeds smuggled by Englishman Henry Wickham, to the Imperial Gardens at Kew and thence to Malaysia, were producing a higher yield. The wild-rubber economy dwindled and the doors to the opera house closed. Over the decades, the French tiles on the dome began to crack, the Italian marble darkened and the fine French furniture and English china slowly began to decay. What you see today is the product of careful restoration, which has returned the *Teatro* to its original glory. There are regular performances, which sell out very quickly, and an arts festival every April.

The Teatro Amazonas sits at the head of a handsome square, the **Praça São Sebastião**, paved with black and white dragon's tooth stones and surrounded by attractive, freshly painted late 19th- and early 20th-century houses. Many are little cafés, galleries or souvenir shops and the area is a safe and pleasant place to while away an hour or two. There are often free concerts on weekend evenings. In the middle of the square is another grand rubber boom construction, the bronze monument to the **Opening of the Ports**. It depicts *Iara* (see Teatro Amazonas, above), embraced by Mercury – representing commerce and standing over five ships, representing the continents of Europe, Africa, America, Oceania and Antarctica. In front of the monument is the modest **Igreja de São Sebastião** ① *R 10 de Julho 567, T092-3232 4572,* whose interior is filled with more brilliantly coloured romantic paintings by Domenico de Angelis, Giancarlo Capranesi (who painted in the Teatro Amazonas and in Belém) and canvases by Bellerini and Francisco Campanella, both also Italian.

Eduardo Ribeiro's house sits on the southwestern edge of the *praça* and opened in 2010 as a museum, the **Museu Casa de Eduardo Ribeiro** ① *R José Clemente s/n, Centro, Mon-Fri 0900-1700, Sun 1600-2100, free guided tours (in Portuguese).* The house is a tall town mansion built in a typically late-Victorian, eclectic style – with a neoclassical façade topped with balcony finished with a Baroque flourish. The two floors of the three-storey interior are devoted to Ribeiro. They are sober when you consider his excesses, bringing together items known to have belonged to the ex-state governor along with photographs, letters and memorabilia, and furniture and decorations from the rubber boom period.

On the waterfront

The city's other sights are huddled around the waterfront. The **Mercado Adolfo Lisboa** ① *R dos Barés 46*, was built in 1882 as a miniature copy of the now-demolished Parisian Les Halles. The wrought ironwork, which forms much of the structure, was imported from Europe and is said to have been designed by Eiffel.

The remarkable harbour installations, completed in 1902, were designed and built by a Scottish engineer to cope with the Rio Negro's annual rise and fall of up to 14 m. The large **floating dock** is connected to street level by a 150-m-long floating ramp, at the end of which, on the harbour wall, can be seen the high-water mark for each year since it was built. The highest so far recorded was in 2009. When the river is high, the roadway floats on a series of large iron tanks measuring 2.5 m in diameter. The large beige **Alfândega (Customs House)** ① *R Marquês de Santa Cruz, Mon-Fri 0800-1300*, stands at the entrance to the city when arriving by boat. Said to be have been modelled on the one in Delhi, it was entirely prefabricated in England, and the tower once acted as a lighthouse.

Dominating the streets between the opera house and the waterfront; and right next to the local bus station, is the **Catedral Municipal**, on Praça Osvaldo Cruz, built in simple Jesuit style and very plain inside and out. Originally constructed in 1695 in wood and straw, it was burnt down in 1850. Nearby is the main shopping and business area, the tree-lined **Avenida Eduardo Ribeiro**, crossed by Avenida 7 de Setembro and bordered by ficus trees.

Some 200 m east of the cathedral is the **Biblioteca Pública (Public Library)** ① *R Barroso 57, T096-3234 0588, Mon-Fri 0730-1730*, inaugurated in 1871, is part of the city's architectural heritage. Featuring an ornate European cast-iron staircase, it is well stocked with 19th-century newspapers, rare books and old photographs, and is worth a visit. Nearby, on the leafy, fountain-filled Praça Heliodoro Balbi (aka Praça da Policia) is a new museum complex, the **Palacete Provincial** ① *Praça Heliodoro Balbi s/n, Centro, T092-3635 5832, Tue-Fri 0900-1700, Sat 1000-1900, Sun 1600-2100, free* . The Palacete is a stately late-19th-century civic palace which was once the police headquarters. It is now home to six small museums: the Museu de Numismática (with a collection on Brazilian and international coins and notes), the Museu Tiradentes (profiling the history of the Amazon police and assorted Brazilian military campaigns), the Museu da Imagem e do Som (with free internet, cinema showings and a DVD library), the Museu de Arqueologia (preserving a handful of Amazon relics), a restoration atelier and the Pinacoteca do Estado – one of the best art galleries in northern Brazil, with work by important painters such as Oscar Ramos, Moacir Andrade and Roberto Burle Marx. The Palacete is a very pleasant place to while away a few hours and has decent air-conditioned café serving tasty coffee, cakes and savouries.

Other museums and cultural centres

The **Museu do Homem do Norte** ① *Av 7 de Setembro 1385, near Av Joaquim Nabuco, T096-3232 5373, Mon-Thu 0900-1200, 1300-1700, Fri 1300-1700, US$1*, is an interesting review of the way of life of the Amazonian population, or 'men of the north', although it has deteriorated in recent years and is now gathering dust. Social, cultural and economic aspects are displayed with photographs, models and other exhibits.

The **Palácio Rio Negro** ① *Av 7 de Setembro 1546, T096-3232 4450, Mon-Fri 0900-1400, free*, was the residence of a German rubber merchant until 1917 whereupon it became the state government palace. It underwent a major refurbishment in 2010 and now has an assortment of rooms presenting potted hagiographies of Amazonas state governors, exhibition spaces and a little café.

The **Museu do Índio** ① *R Duque de Caxias 296, near Av 7 Setembro, T096-234 1422, Tue-Fri 0930-1730, Sat, Sun and holidays 1300-1700, US$1.70, free on Sun*, is managed by the Salesian missionaries who have been responsible for the ravaging of much of the indigenous culture of the upper Rio Negro. It is rather run down and betrays a Victorian view of indigenous culture. The displays are dusty and poorly displayed, but there are plenty of artefacts, including handicrafts, ceramics, clothing, utensils and ritual objects from the various indigenous tribes of the upper Rio Negro. There is also a small craft shop.

West of the centre

The **Instituto Geográfico e Histórico do Amazonas** ① *R Frei José dos Inocentes 132, Manaus, T092-3622 1260, Mon-Fri 0900-1200 and 1300-1600, US$1.50*, is located in the oldest part of Manaus – a cluster of streets of tiny cottages dotted with grand, rubber boom buildings. It houses a museum and library of over 10,000 books, which thoroughly document Amazonian life through the ages.

The **Zoo** ① *Estrada Ponta Negra 750, T096-625 2044, Tue-Sun 0900-1630, US$3, free on Sun, take bus No 120 from R Tamandaré by the cathedral, US$0.70, every 30 mins, get off 400 m past the 1st infantry barracks*, a big white building, is run by CIGS, the Brazilian Army Unit specializing in jungle survival. It has recently been expanded and improved. About 300 Amazonian animals are kept in the gardens, including anacondas in a huge pit.

Further afield

The **Bosque da Ciência INPA** are maintained by the **Instituto Nacional de Pesquisas da Amazônia (INPA)** ① *R Otavio Cabral, Petropolis, T092-3643 3293, US$3, Tue-Fri 0900-1130, 1400-1630, Sat and Sun 0900-1630, take bus No 519 from the Praça da Matriz*, which conducts research into all aspects of the Amazon. There is a small park that is good for rainforest flora and fauna before you head out to the forest. The animals here are kept in less distressing conditions than in the city zoo. Paca (*Agouti paca*), agouti (*Myoprocta exilis*), squirrel monkeys (*Saimiri scicureus*) and tamarins (*Saguinus sp*) roam free, and among the other animals on display are Amazonian manatee (*Trichechus inunguis*) and giant otter (*Pternura brasiliensis*). A small museum within the park has displays on indigenous peoples use of the forest, medicinal plants and bottles of pickled poisonous snakes. INPA also manages what is probably the largest urban rainforest reserve in the world, on the northeastern edge of Manaus. Pedro Fernandes Neto (T092-9090 9983, pedroffneto@hotmail.com), takes guided tours and other activities in and around the city. This is far more interesting than the Jardim Botânico Chico Mendes, which isn't really worth visiting.

The **Centro Cultural dos Povos da Amazônia** ① *Praça Francisco Pereira da Silva s/n, Bola da Suframa, Centro, T092-2125 5300, www.ccpa.am.gov.br*, is a large cultural complex devoted to the indigenous peoples of the Amazon. Outside the building there are Desano and a Yanomami *maloca* (traditional buildings), and the large, modern and well-curated museum in the main building preserves many artefacts, including splendid headdresses, ritual clothing and weapons. Explanatory displays are in Portuguese and passable English. It's a far better museum than the old-fashioned Museu do Indio. There are also play areas for the kids, a library and internet.

There is a curious little church, **Igreja do Pobre Diabo**, at the corner of Avenida Borba and Avenida Ipixuna, in the suburb of Cachoeirinha. It is only 4 m wide by 5 m long, and was built by a local trader, the 'poor devil' of the name. To get there, take the 'Circular 7 de Setembro Cachoeirinha' bus from the cathedral to Hospital Militar.

The **Museu de Ciências Naturais da Amazônia (Natural Science Museum)** ① *Av Cosme Ferreira, Cachoeira Grande suburb, 15 km from centre, T092-3644 2799, Mon-Sat 0900-1200 and 1400-1700, US$6, best to combine with a visit to INPA, and take a taxi from there (see above)*, is one of the city's little-known treasures. The remote museum is run by Japanese, with characteristic efficiency, and the exhibits are beautifully displayed and clearly labelled in Japanese, Portuguese and English. The main building houses hundreds of preserved Amazon insects and butterflies, together with stuffed specimens of a selection of the river's bizarre fish. You can also see live versions, including the endangered pirarucu (*Arapaima gigas*), which can grow up to 3.5 m, and a primitive osteoglottid fish that breathes air.

Beaches

Manaus has two sandy beaches on the outskirts of the city. The **Praia da Ponta Negra**, which lies upstream of the city's pollution, is the most popular and the most heavily developed. It is backed by high-rise flats and lined with open-air restaurants, bars and areas for beach volleyball and football. Nightlife here is lively, especially at weekends. However, on most nights at least one of the bars (such as **O Laranjinha**, see page 93) will have Boi Bumba dance shows. Many of the better hotels, including the **Tropical**, are situated here. To get here take any bus marked 'Ponta Negra' (eg No 120) from the local bus station next to the cathedral. The beach can also be reached on the Tropical's shuttle bus (see page 88). Boats also leave from here for other beaches on the Rio Negro.

The meeting of the waters

About 15 km from Manaus is the confluence of the coffee-coloured **Rio Solimões** (Amazon) and the black-tea coloured **Rio Negro**, which is itself some 8 km wide. The two rivers run side by side for about 6 km without their waters mingling. This phenomenon is caused by differences in the temperature, density and velocity of the two rivers. Tourist agencies run boat trips to this spot (US$60-160). The simplest route is to take a taxi, or bus No 713 'Vila Buriti', to the Porto de CEASA dock, and take the car ferry across to Careiro. Ferries leave all the time when full and there are many other smaller boats too. The last departure from CEASA is at 1800 and the last return to CEASA from Careiro is 2000. Motor boats for the meeting of the water charge US$15 per person or US$80 per boat (up to five people). Boats also leave from the hotel **Tropical** (US$90 per boat, up to five people). You should see dolphins, especially in the early morning. Alternatively, hire a motorized canoe from near the market in the city centre (about US$30; per person or US$180 per boat for up to eight people). Allow three to four hours to experience the meeting properly. A 2-km walk along the Porto Velho road from the CEASA ferry terminal leads to some ponds, some way from the road, in which huge Victoria Regia water lilies can be seen from April to September.

Around Manaus

Museu Seringal

ⓘ *Igarapé São João, 15 km north of Manaus up the Rio Negro, Tue-Sun 0800-1600, T092-3234 8755, US$3 and US$15 round trip on a private launch from the Hotel Tropical.* This museum sitting at the end of a pretty *igarapé* (creek) off the Rio Negro is a full-scale reproduction of an early 20th-century rubber-tapping mansion house, with serf quarters, a factory and a shop complete with authentic products. It was built as a film set for the 2002 Portuguese feature film, *A Selva*. A guided tour – especially from one of the former rubber tappers brings home the full horror of the system of debt peonage that enslaved Brazilians up until the 1970s. The museum can be visited with **Amazon Flower** or **Amazon Gero Tours**.

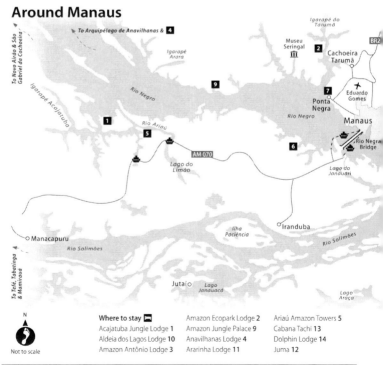

Around Manaus

Where to stay 🛏
Acajatuba Jungle Lodge **1**
Aldeia dos Lagos Lodge **10**
Amazon Antônio Lodge **3**
Amazon Ecopark Lodge **2**
Amazon Jungle Palace **9**
Anavilhanas Lodge **4**
Ararinha Lodge **11**
Ariaú Amazon Towers **5**
Cabana Tachi **13**
Dolphin Lodge **14**
Juma **12**

Arquipélago de Anavilhanas

This filigree of more than 350 brilliant-green islands in the jet-black Rio Negro – some fringed with white-sand beaches, others anchored only by their roots – is one of the area's must-see sights. The scene is particularly beautiful at the end of the day when the sky looks vast and warm and the light on the trunks of the partially submerged trees is a thick orange-yellow. Birds fly into the Anavilhanas to roost and millions of bats leave for their night hunt. The air is silent but for bird calls, the lapping of the river and the bluster of river dolphins surfacing for air. The islands are 80 km upstream of Manaus. Several companies arrange visits to the archipelago (US$195-285, per person, one day – it takes four hours to reach the islands), as can most of the Rio Negro lodges. Rio Negro safari cruises almost all visit the Anavilhanas.

It is possible to see botos (pink river dolphins) being fed, and even to swim with them at the **Boto Cor-de-Rosa restaurant** in the Anavilhanas village of Novo Airão. Visits should be booked through a Manaus tour operator in as small a group as possible.

Presidente Figueiredo

There are hundreds of waterfalls dotted through the forest and scrubby savannah that surrounds the sleepy town of Presidente Figueiredo, 117 km north of Manaus on the shores of the vast artificial lake Balbina, formed by the ill-fated Figueiredo dam. It's possible to visit three or four on a day trip from Manaus. With an overnight stay it's also possible to see the beautiful and (in Brazil) very rare Guianan Cock of the Rock (Rupicola rupicola). This is one of South America's most spectacular sights. Males are pigeon-sized, and brilliant tangerine, with an exuberant, almost iridescent half-moon crest which completely obscures the beak, an orange-tipped black tail and silky-orange filaments which stick out at bizarre angles around the wings and tail. Females are a dull brown with a yellow-tipped black bill. Up to 40 males at a time perform elaborate courtship dances for the females in forest clearings called *leks*, twisting and trilling and displaying their extraordinary crests until a female settles behind her chosen mate and pecks him on the rump. Cock of the rocks can only be seen on an organized tour (see page 95).

Figueiredo has so many waterfalls and caves, it's hard to know where to begin. The most spectacular are arguably the following: **Cachoeira Gruta da Judeia**, which plummets

Pousada dos
Guanavenas **8**
Tiwa Amazone Resort **6**
Tropical **7**

Tropical Business **7**
Zequinha Lodge **15**

off the lip of a gargantuan cave in the forest; **Cachoeira Arco Iris** and **Cachoeira Iracema** which are a series of stepped falls plunging through rocky gorges and over huge boulders; and **Cachoeira Pedra Furada**, which rushes through a series of holes in an enormous rock. Activities include abseiling, canyoning and whitewater rafting; ask for Johnny (bookable through **Pedro Neto** – see Guides, page 96), who organizes these around Figueiredo.

Presidente Figueiredo town – often called **Balbina** – is an uninteresting place, built in the 1970s as a settlers' camp for construction workers on the dam. Its grid of streets lead to a long beach which gets packed with visitors from Manaus at weekends and a small centre for rehabilitating distressed Amazonian manatees (intermittently open).

Presidente Figueiredo's attractions are spread out over a large area, and whilst even the remotest falls are no more than two hours walk off a road, driving distances are long and there is no public transport. The only practical way to visit Figueiredo is with a hire car from Manaus, or on an organized tour with an operator in Manaus. If you are passing through on the way to or from Boa Vista, trips can be organized through the **Pousada das Pedras** or the **Pousada Wal** in Balbina. There are at least six buses a day to Balbina from the Manaus *rodoviária*. Boa Vista buses will stop at Balbina on request.

Downstream from Manaus → *For listings, see pages 88-100.*

Parintins → *Phone code: 092. Population: 90,000.*
Parintins is situated between Manaus and Santarém, just before the Amazonas-Pará border, on the Ilha Tupinambana. In the dry season, boat trips run to the river beaches and to nearby lakes. The **airport** ① *Estrada Odovaldo Novo s/n, Parintins, T092-3533 2700*, receives flights from Manaus, Óbidos and Santarém and others. Boats stop here on the Belém–Manaus route. there are also sailings from Óbidos and Santarém. ►► *See Transport, page 99.*

In colonial times, this was the resting point of a group of coastal indigenous Brazilians who made an astonishing trek through thousands of miles of dense forest to escape the ravages of the Portuguese slave trade. However, they didn't evade it for long. Within a generation they had been found by slavers from Belém who took all the women and children and murdered all the men. Ironically the island is now the site of one of the country's most important and spectacular festivals, Boi Bumba, which celebrates the triumph of the indigenous and *caboclo* poor over a *coronel* (tyrannical landowner).

The **Festa do Boi Bumba** (see box opposite) is the most vibrant in Brazil after Carnaval and draws tens of thousands of visitors to Parintins on the last three days of June each year. But since the town has only two small hotels, finding a room can be a challenge. Everyone sleeps in hammocks on the boats that bring them to the festival from Manaus and Santarém (a large vessel will charge US$130 per person, including breakfast).

Upstream from Manaus → *For listings, see pages 88-100.*

Tefé and the Mamirauá Ecological Reserve → *Phone code: 097. Population: 65,000.*
Tefé is a scruffy town roughly halfway between Manaus and the Colombian border. The local airport authorities confiscated all of the city's rubbish lorries in a dispute over the municipal dump, and now it is piled up willy-nilly. But few come here for the town itself,

Festa do Boi Bumba

The Boi Bumba festival in Parintins is a competition between two rival groups, similar to the samba schools in Rio, called Caprichoso (whose colour is blue) and Garantido (red). The two teams present a pageant, which originates from Braga in Portugal, but has been heavily syncretized with indigenous and Afro-Brazilian themes. It was brought to Parintins in the early 20th century by settlers from São Luís in Maranhão. The pageant tells the story of Pai Francisco and his wife Mãe Catirina who steal the prize bull from the landowner that they work for, and kill it. The landowner discovers this and threatens to kill them if they fail to resurrect his bull by midnight. The couple employ the talents of a shaman, a priest and an African *pai santo*, and these characters invoke the female spirit of rainforest fertility, the Cunhã-poranga, played by a beautiful young dancer. The story is told to the backdrop of vast four-storey floats with moving parts and troupes of hundreds of dancers. It is performed in the purpose-built *bumbódromo* stadium which holds almost 40,000 spectators. Previews of the festival in miniature are held in the **Hotel Tropical** in Manaus throughout the year and there are always Boi Bumba dancers on weekend evenings in the Ponta Negra bars in Manaus.

for this is the access point to one of the world's most important primate and waterfowl reserves, the **Mamirauá Ecological Reserve** ⓘ *T097-3343 4160, www.mamiraua.org.br and www.uakarilodge.com.br*. This is a Ramsar, www.ramsar.org, site set up with British support to protect huge areas of terra firme, gallery, *varzea* and *igapó* forest at the confluence of the Solimões and Japurá rivers, and to manage them sustainably with the local riverine people. There are abundant birds including numerous rare trogons, cotingas, currasows, hoatzin, harpy eagle and five species of macaw. There are black caiman (one of which lives under the floating lodge), both species of Amazon dolphin, and numerous rare primates – the most spectacular of which are the endemic black-headed squirrel monkey and the endangered white uakari, known locally as the 'macaco Ingles' because of its red complexion and its genitalia. A visit is unforgettable.

The reserve has a small floating lodge, the **Pousada Uacari** (see page 91) on the Mamirauá river and visitors stay here in simple but elegant wooden rooms. Trips include walks in terra firme forest, boat and canoe trips to *igarpe* creeks, *varzea* and *igapó* forest and the vast Mamirauá lake. Visits must be booked in advance.

Tefé is connected to Manaus by air daily, with onward flights to Tabatinga. There are regular slow boats (at least one a day) from Manaus or from Tabatinga and fast speed boats from Manaus (see page 98). The town is small enough to negotiate on foot.

Border with Colombia and Peru

Benjamin Constant → *Phone code: 097. Population: 23,000.*
This tiny town, with a big sawmill and a series of little tiled houses set in bougainvillea gardens, sits on the frontier with Peru, just opposite Leticia in Colombia. There is an

interesting **Ticuna indigenous cultural centre and museum** ⓘ *Av Castelo Branco 396, T096-415 5624*, with artefacts, information panels and a gift shop. The music is haunting but sadly not for sale. Ticuna people run the museum.

There are boat services from Manaus (seven days or more), to Manaus (four days or more) and from Iquitos in Peru. There are no facilities in Benjamin Constant, but it is possible to buy supplies for boat journeys. Benjamin Constant is two hours from Tabatinga and Leticia (ferry/*recreio* US$2; 25 minutes by speedboat, US$4 per person, cheaper if more passengers). ▶▶ *For boats to/from Manaus, see Routes in Amazônia, page 97.*

Tabatinga → *Phone code: 097. Population: 38,000.*

Tabatinga is theoretically 4 km from Leticia (in Colombia) but, in reality, it is the scruffy half of the same town: a long street buzzing with mopeds, a port and some untidy houses in between. There is an important Ticuna centre here, and the town is the headquarters of one of the country's most important indigenous NGOs, **FIUPAM**, fiupam@yahoo.com.br. However, there is little of interest for tourists, who are better off staying in Leticia. Flights arrive in Leticia (see below) from where a minibus to Tabatinga costs US$1.

The port area in Tabatinga is called Marco and the port captain is very helpful and speaks good English. There are regular boats from Manaus and from Benjamin Constant, across the water, and from Iquitos in Peru. A mosquito net for a hammock is essential if sailing upstream from Tabatinga, much less so downstream. A good hammock will cost US$15 in Tabatinga (try **Esplanada Teocides**).

Travel between Tabatinga and Leticia (Colombia) is very informal. Taxis between the towns charge US$5 (more if you want to stop at immigration offices or change money), or US$0.80 in a *colectivo* (more after 1800). Beware of taxi drivers who want to rush you expensively over the border before it 'closes'. It is not advisable to walk the muddy path between Tabatinga and Leticia as robberies occur here. Boats from Manaus normally start from Tabatinga and spend a day or two here before returning; you can stay on board. ▶▶ *For boats to/from Manaus, see Routes in Amazônia, page 97.*

Leticia (Colombia) → *International phone code +57. Phone code: 9859.*

This riverside city is clean and modern, though run down, and is rapidly merging into one town with neighbouring Marco in Brazil. Leticia is a good place to buy indigenous products typical of the Amazon, and tourist services are better than in Tabatinga or Benjamin Constant. The best time to visit the area is in July or August, the early months of the dry season. At weekends, accommodation may be difficult to find.

The **museum** ⓘ *Cra 11 y Calle 9*, set up by **Banco de la República**, covers local ethnography and archaeology and is set in a beautiful building with a library and a terrace overlooking the Amazon. There is a small **Amazonian zoo** ⓘ *US$1*, and botanical garden on the road to the airport, within walking distance of town (20 minutes).

The **airport** ⓘ *1.5 km from town*, receives flights from Manaus (three times a week with Rico) via Tefé. It is a small terminal with few facilities. A taxi to the centre costs US$1.60. There is a **tourist office** ⓘ *C 10, No 9-86, Ministerio del Medio Ambiente, Cra 11, No 12-05*, for general information on national parks.

Up the Rio Negro

It is possible to get a public passenger boat from São Raimundo port on the outskirts of Manaus up the Rio Negro (see Routes in Amazônia, page 97). There are hardly any villages of more than a few houses, but these places are important in terms of communications and food resources. It is vital to be self-sufficient in terms of food and cash and to be able to speak Portuguese or have a Brazilian guide. **Nova Airão**, on the west bank of the Negro, next to the southern extremity of the Anavilhanas islands, is a three-hour bus trip across the newly opened Rio Negro road bridge. It has a large boat-building centre at the south end, and a fish and vegetable market at the north end. Ice and bread can also be purchased here. It has a telephone, from which international calls can usually be made. There is road access and a bus service from Manaus.

North of Nova Airão and 220 km from Manaus on the Rio Negro, is the UNESCO World Heritage-listed **Parque Nacional Jaú**. This is Brazil's largest national park and, at 2,272,000 ha, is the largest protected area of tropical forest in the world. It encompasses the entire Jáu river basin, from its headwaters to its source. The only way to get here is with a tour; there is no transport or facilities (guides or tour operators charge US200-230 per person per day for a minimum of four people). Permits are necessary. Guides and operators can organize these or you can contact the Instituto Chico Mendes de Conservação da Biodiversidade (ICMBio) ⓘ *www.icmbio.gov.br*. Like most Brazilian parks, Jaú is a paper park – meaning that whilst it is delineated on the map it is not policed or practically protected. However, it is, in the main, pristine wilderness. The park is little visited and little studied but, according to ICMBio, so far they have recorded 400 species of vascular plants, a number of which are endemic; 263 species of fish (almost half as many as the entire continent of Europe); and all the large terrestrial Amazonian mammals.

Moura is about five days upstream from Manaus. It has basic medical facilities and the military base has an airstrip (only usable September to December) and tele-communications. About a day further upstream is **Carvoeira**, almost opposite the mouth of the Rio Branco. There is a vibrant festival in the first week of August. A couple of days beyond is **Barcelos**, with a daily air service, except Sundays, the centre for bass fishing on the Amazon. There are a couple of places to stay here.

São Gabriel da Cachoeira and on towards Venezuela

A great distance further upstream is São Gabriel da Cachoeira, some 900 km and 10 days from Manaus by boat. The city is tiny and sits under a hulking mountain in front of a series of dramatic rapids. There are fine white-sand beaches on the Negro during the dry season. São Gabriel is near the **Pico da Neblina National Park**, named after the highest mountain in Brazil (3014 m). Visit the park with **Roraima Adventures** in Boa Vista, see page 104.

There are flights four times a week with **Trip**, www.airtrip.com.br. You can continue from São Gabriel to Venezuela or to Colombia; be sure to get an exit stamp for Brazil here and an entry stamp for Colombia. Visas for Venezuela must be obtained in Manaus. There is a Colombian consulate in São Gabriel near the **FOIRN** indigenous headquarters. In São Gabriel there are two banks but no exchange facilities and the **Vaupes** hotel (**$**). Cargo boats go to **Cucuí** at the border between Brazil, Colombia and Venezuela. There is also a twice-weekly bus, US$5 (one hotel, ask for Elias, no restaurants). From Cucuí there are daily boats to Guadalupe (Colombia) and infrequent boats to Santa Lucía (Venezuela).

Amazonas and the Amazon River listings

For hotel and restaurant price codes and other relevant information, see pages 10-13.

Where to stay

Manaus *p75, map p75*

Whilst there are a number of hostels and cheap guesthouses, Manaus lacks hotels of quality in the Centro Histórico. The best establishments are in Ponta Negra or close to the airport; both very inconvenient for seeing almost all that is interesting in the city. The best area to stay in the city centre is around the **Teatro Amazonas**, where the Italianate colonial houses and cobbled squares have been newly refurbished. Although the area around Av Joaquim Nabuco and R dos Andradas has lots of cheap hotels, this is a low-key red-light district which is very sketchy at night, as is the Zona Franca – around the docks. Things are expected to change in the years approaching the World Cup.

$$$$ Tropical, Av Coronel Teixeira 1320, Ponta Negra, T092-3659 5000, www.tropical hotel.com.br. A lavish though increasingly frayed 5-star hotel 20 km outside the city in a semi-forested parkland setting next to the river. The hotel has a private beach, tennis court and a large pool with wave machine. There are several restaurants including a decent *churrascaria*. The river dock is a departure point for many river cruises. To get here take a Ponta Negra bus from the Praça da Matriz, US$1.50, then walk or take a taxi. A taxi to the centre costs around US$30. Service can be slow. There is a hotel tour agency.

$$$$ Tropical Business, Av Coronel Teixeira 1320, Ponta Negra, T092-2123 3000, www.tropicalhotel.com.br. The business companion to the **Tropical**, just a few doors away, is far better, cleaner and more contemporary. Rooms and suites are modern and well appointed, housed in a large tower block with great views out over the river

from the upper floors. The hotel has the best business facilities in the city and has a lovely infinity pool set in gardens overlooking the beach. Like the other hotels in Ponta Negra, it's a long way from the centre.

$$$ Ana Cássia Palace, R dos Andradas 14, Centre, T092-3303 3637, www.anacassia.com.br. Faded, poorly renovated, unsecure, but bright and spacious rooms, some with great views of the port. The hotel has a rooftop restaurant and breakfast area and a pool.

$$$ Lord Manaus, R Marcílio Dias 217, T092-3622 2844, www.lordmanaus.com.br. Pleasant, spacious lobby and standard a/c rooms with writing desks and beds, all of which are in some need of refurbishment. Conveniently located for boats and shops, in the heart of the Zona Franca but it is not safe to walk around this area at night.

$$$ Manaós, Av Eduardo Ribeiro 881, T092-3633 5744, www.hotelmanaos.com.br. Recently renovated and right next to the Teatro Amazonas. Spruce a/c rooms with marble floors and smart bathrooms. Decent breakfast.

$$$ Taj Mahal Hotel, Av Getúlio Vargas 741, Centre, T092-3627 3737. A large, business hotel in a superb location overlooking the Opera House in the city centre. Facilities include a revolving rooftop restaurant and a spa. The hotel could be one of the city's best but it's looking very, very tired nowadays, and the staff seem equally so. Rooms and public areas are in sore need of refurbishment, but this is one of the very few hotels in the centre it's possible to reserve through email.

$$$-$$ Go Inn, R Monsenhor Coutinho 560, Centro Histórico, T092-3306 2600, www.atlanticahotels.com.br. This 2010 opening is one of the very few decent, modern a/c accommodation options in the city centre – with undistinguished but no-nonsense corporate-designed rooms with tiny desks, queen-sized beds and wall-mounted TVs. Facilities include a café, disabled rooms, gym and paid Wi-Fi in all rooms.

$$ Central, R Dr Moreira 202, T092-3622 2609, www.hotelcentralmanaus.com.br. A business hotel tucked away behind the Palacete Provincial, with a range of rooms, many very scruffy although some well kept; look at a few. Excellent large breakfast.

$$ Krystal, R Barroso 54, T092-3233 7535, www.krystalhotel.com.br. Small, boxy a/c rooms in soft colours, with polished tile floors, TVs a fridge and wardrobe and little else.

$$ Lider, Av 7 de Setembro 827, T092-3621 9700, www.liderhotelmanaus.com.br. Small modern a/c rooms with marble floors, little breakfast tables and en suite bathrooms. The best are at the front of the hotel on the upper floors. Very well kept.

$$-$ Brasil, Av Getúlio Vargas 657, T092-2101 5000, hotel-brasil@internext.com.br. Faded cavernous a/c rooms decorated with tacky art and with tiny en suite bathrooms and even tinier balconies. Small pool.

$ Dez de Julho, R 10 de Julho 679, T092-3232 6280, www.hoteldezdejulho.com. One of the better cheap option, with clean though simple rooms (some with a/c and hot water). One of the best tour operators (**Amazon Gero**) in the lobby and efficient, English-speaking staff. In a great location next to Praça São Sebastião.

$ Hostel Manaus, R Lauro Cavalcante 231, Centro, T092-3233 4545, www.hostelmanaus.com. Cheaper for HI members. HI hostel in one of the city's original houses. Good-value dorms and private rooms. Quiet and reasonably central with views of the city from the rooftop patio. Australian-run. Great place to join a jungle tour – with a good tour operator in the lobby (see below). Not to be confused with a non-HI hostel in the city using a similar name.

Lodges accessible from Manaus

When reserved in advance, either direct or through an operator (see page 95), lodges will organize all transfers from either a Manaus hotel or in many cases the airport.

$$$$ Acajatuba Jungle Lodge, Lago Acajatuba, 4 hrs up the Rio Negro from Manaus. Office at Av 7 de Setembro 1899, Manaus, T092-3234 3199, www.acajatuba.com.br. This Rio Negro lodge sits in a beautiful location on the edge of Acajatuba lake – a large igarapé visited by boto dolphins, at the far southern end of the Anavilhanas islands. 40 apartments, a bar and a restaurant. Accommodation is in simple, round, thatched roof bungalows with mosquito screens (but no nets – bring your own). The lodge does not conform to best ecotourism practice – guides handle wild animals.

$$$$ Amazon Jungle Palace, office at R Emilio Moreira 470, Manaus, T092-3212 5600, www.amazonjunglepalace.com.br. A floating lodge with very comfortable a/c 4-star rooms and a pool, on a black-water tributary of the Rio Negro some 5 km from the Anavilhanas. Excellent guides and service but, as ever with lodges close to Manaus, somewhat depleted forest.

$$$$ Anavilhanas Lodge, Edifício Manaus Shopping Centre, Av Eduardo Ribeiro 520, sala 304, T092-3622 8996, www.anavilhanaslodge.com. This is the nearest jungle lodges get to boutique. Minimalist rooms with high thread count cotton on the beds, low-lighting, flatscreen TVs and tasteful rustic chic hangings and decor sit in thatch-roofed cabins whose front walls are entirely glass-fronted – giving spectacular views out over the Rio Negro and the adjacent Anavilhanas archipelago. There's a lodge bar serving *cupuaçu* caipirinhas, amongst other drinks, and a range of comfortable lounging areas. But bring a mosquito net. The large menu of activities includes the standard piranha fishing, community visits, hikes and dolphin spotting alongside more meditative kayaking and sunset tours of the Anavilhanas.

$$$$ Ariaú Amazon Towers, 60 km and 2 hrs by boat from Manaus, on the Rio Ariaú, 2 km from Archipélago de Anavilhanas; office at R Leonardo Malcher 699, Manaus, T092-2121 5000, www.ariautowers.com.br. With 271 rooms in complex of towers connected by walkways, a pool, meditation centre, large restaurant and gift shop, this is a jungle hotel more than a jungle lodge. If you are after intimacy with the forest you won't find it here. But the hotel is a good option for older people or those with small children. The guided tours are generally well run, although specialist wildlife guides are not available and tame wildlife hangs around the lodge.

$$$$ Pousada dos Guanavenas, Ilha de Silves, 300 km from Manaus on the road to Itacoatiara, then by boat along the Rio Urubu. T092-3656 1500, www.guanavenas.net, A large lodge in cleared grounds overlooking the black-water Lago Canacari, some 4-5 hrs from Manaus. The hotel has a pool, excellent restaurant and very comfortable a/c rooms with hot water. The hotel's tours run like clockwork – sometimes too much so.

$$$$-$$$ Amazon Ecopark Lodge, Igarapé do Tarumã, 20 km from Manaus, 15 mins by boat, T092-2547 7742 or T092-9146 0594 www.amazonecopark.com.br. The best lodge within an hour of Manaus, in a private forest that would otherwise have been deforested. The lodge makes a real effort at conservation and good practice. The apartment cabins are very comfortable (hot showers) and set in the forest. The lodge has a lovely white-sand beach and is close to the **Amazon Monkey Jungle**, an ecological park where primate species (including white uakari) are treated and rehabilitated in natural surroundings. The **Living Rainforest Foundation**, which administers the ecopark, also offers educational jungle trips and overnight camps (bring your own food), entrance US$20.

$$$ Ararinha Lodge, Paraná do Araçá, exclusively through **Amazon Gero Tours**, www.amazongerotours.com. One of the more comfortable lodges in the Mamori area. This lodge sits on a riverbank overlooking the Paraná do Araça – a little visited and unspoilt river running off the Lago do Mamori lake regions. Accommodation is in smart wooden chalets housing suites of individual rooms which come complete with double or single beds with mosquito nets. The area is one of the best for wildlife in the Mamori region.

$$$ Dolphin Lodge, Paraná do Mamori, T092-3877 9247, through **Maia Expeditions**, www.maiaexpeditions.com. A small lodge with simple wooden cabins perched on a grassy bluff overlooking the Parana do Mamori river (off Lago Mamori). The lodge runs tours and has kayaks for guests to use.

$$$ Juma, Lago da Juma, T092-3232 2707, www.jumalodge.com. A newly refurbished lodge in a beautiful location on the outer reaches of Lago Mamori at Juma. Accommodation is in comfortable wooden and palm-thatch huts on stilts right on the riverbank. The owners have a burgeoning interest in birdwatching and proper wildlife tours.

$$$ Tiwa Amazone Resort, Lago Salvador, 10 mins across the Rio Negro from Ponta Negra, T092-3088 4676, T092-9995 7892, www.tiwaamazone.com. A medium-sized resort lodge with comfortable spacious cabanas with en suites and a/c, built out over a small caiman-filled lake. The resort has a large pool and bar. Too close to Manaus for much wildlife, but an option as an alternative city hotel, especially for a business trip. Good tours.

$$$-$$ Aldeia dos Lagos Lodge, near Silves, run by the **Silves Project**, T092-3248 9988, through **Viverde** tours (see page 95), www.aldeiadoslagos.com. A community-based eco-project run in conjunction with an NGO. Accommodation is in a simple floating lodge set in a system of lakes near the tiny town of Silves and with high environmental diversity. Good for birds and caiman. Profits are fed back into local communities.

$$$-$$ Amazon Antônio Jungle Lodge, through **Antonio Jungle Tours**, www.antonio-jungletours.com. A thatched roof wooden lodge with plain, fan-cooled wooden rooms and an observation tower. Set in a beautiful location overlooking a broad curve in the river Urubu 200 km from Manaus.

$$ Cabana Tachi, through **Amazon Jungle Tours**, T092-9627 4151, www.amazonjungle tours.com. A simple, rustic community- owned lodge run in ecotourism partnership with **Amazon Gero Tours** in a pioneering project where money and resources return to the community. In one of the most pristine stretches of forest in the region. Good wildlife.

$$ Zequinha, through **Amazon Gero Tours**, www.amazongerotours.com. Very simple wooden fan-cooled rooms and 1 a/c suite in a round maloca building 100 m from a bluff overlooking the Lago Mamori.

Presidente Figueiredo *p83*
$$ Pousada das Pedras, Av Acariquara 2, Presidente Figueiredo, T092-3324 1296, www.pousadadaspedras.am.com.br. Simple tiled rooms in a tropical garden, a generous breakfast of fruit, rolls, juices and coffee and tours organized to waterfalls and caves by the enthusiastic owner.

$$ Pousada do Wal, BR-174, T092-3324 1267, www.pousadadawal.com.br. A pretty little *pousada* with terracotta-tile and whitewashed bungalows set in a little garden pation off a quiet Balbina street. Rooms are very simple with TVs, fridges, simple wooden furnishings and a bed, and public areas are strung with hammocks. The hotel can help organize excursions.

Tefé *p84*
$$$$ Pousada Uacari, T097-3343 4672 or T097-3343 4160, www.uakarilodge.com.br. This is the best lodge for wildlife, guiding and

ecotouristic practice in the Brazilian Amazon. The lodge is in a magical location in the Mamirauá reserve, floating on a river, with 10 suites of 25 sq m each linked by floating bridges. Tours are excellent. Look out for the friendly black caiman which lives in the water under the restaurant. The lodge and trips in the reserve can be booked in Manaus via **Iguana Tours**, either at their shop or office in Manaus airport. Book well in advance.

$ Anilce, Praça Santa Teresa 294. Clean, a/c, very helpful. Don't leave valuables in your room.

$ Hotel Panorama, R Floriano Peixoto 90. Recommended, with a good restaurant.

Benjamin Constant *p85*

There are a number of very cheap and very simple *pousadas* in town.

$$ Benjamin Constant, R Getúlio Vargas 36, beside the ferry, T092-3415 5638; postal address Apdo Aéreo 219, Leticia, Colombia. All rooms have a/c, some with hot water and TV. Good restaurant, arranges tours.

Tabatinga *p86*

$$ Pousada do Sol, General Sampaio, T092-3412 3355. Simple rooms but in a hotel with a sauna and a pool. Friendly owners.

$ Travellers Jungle Home, R Marechal Rondon 86. A little hostel and tour operator with Brazilian/French owners and a pet snake.

Leticia (Colombia) *p86*

The international phone code for Colombia is +57. The code for Leticia is 9819.

$$$ Anaconda, Cra 11 No 7-34, T9819-27119. The plushest in town with large a/c rooms, hot water, a restaurant and pool.

$$ Colonial, Cra 10 No 7-08, T9819-27164. A/c or fans, pool, cafeteria, noisy.

$$-$ Residencias Fernando, Cra 9, No 8-80, T9819-27362. Simple but well appointed and clean. Recommended.

$ Residencia Internacional, Av Internacional, between the centre and the Brazilian border. Basic rooms with attached bathrooms and fans. Hard beds.

$ Residencias La Manigua, C 8 No 9-22, T9819-27121. Friendly staff and modest but well-maintained rooms.

$ Residencias Marina, Cra 9 No 9-29, T9819-26014. Standard cheap hotel rooms, TV, some with a/c, cold water, good breakfast and meals at attached restaurant.

Restaurants

Manaus *p75, map p75*

Many restaurants close Sun night and Mon. The best are a 10-15-min taxi ride from the Centro Histórico.

$$$ Banzeiro, R Libertador 102, Adrianópolis, T092-9204 7056, www.restaurante banzeiro.com.br. Chef Ivar Schaedler cooks gourmet traditional Amazonian and Brazilian dishes, served in a pretty dining room. 10-min taxi ride from the Centro Histórico. Dishes include *pato no tucupi* (see page 12) and *caldeirinha de tucanaré* (peacock bass fish broth). Delicious drinks include *batidas de cacau* (made with the chocolate bean fruit) and *caipiroska amazonica* (with *cupuacu*).

$$$ Village, R Mario Ypiranga Monteiro 948, Adrianópolis, T092-3234 3296, www.villagerestaurante.com.br. The favourite dining room of Manaus' burgeoning wealthy elite is a contemporary space flooded with warm natural light through big glass windows or low-lit for intimate after-dark dining. The best options from the big menu are the river fish and regional dishes.

$$$-$$ Himawari, R 10 de Julho 618, opposite Teatro Amazonas, T092-3233 2208. A conveniently located a/c Japanese restaurant serving reasonable sushi, sashimi, steamed pastries and salads by Teruko Sakai who was born and spent his early years in Nagasaki. Attentive service, good sake and open Sun night when many restaurants close.

$$ Búfalo, Av Joaquim Nabuco 628, T092-3633 3733, www.churrascariabufalo.com.br.

The best *churrascaria* in Manaus, with a US$12 all-you-can-eat Brazilian BBQ and a vast choice of meat. Come with an empty stomach.

$$ Canto da Peixada, R Emílio Moreira 1677 (Praça 14 de Janeiro), T092-3234 3021. One of the longest-established *peixadas* (simple fresh fish restaurants) in Manaus. Unpretentious, always vibrant and with excellent Amazon fishes from Jaraqui to Tambaqui. A short taxi ride from the centre.

$$ Fiorentina, R José Paranaguá 44, Praça da Polícia, T092-3232 1295. Fan-cooled traditional Italian with cheesy vegetarian dishes and even cheesier piped music. Great *feijoada* on Sat, half-price on Sun. Dishes are served with mugs of wine.

$$ Pizzeria Scarola, R 10 de Julho 739, corner with Av Getúlio Vargas, T092-3232 6503. Standard menu and pizza delivery, popular.

$ Alemã, R José Paranaguá, Praça da Polícia. Food by weight with great pastries, hamburgers, juices, sandwiches.

$ Senac, R Saldanha Marinho 644, T092-3633 2277. Lunch only. Cookery school with a self-service restaurant. Highly recommended.

$ Skina dos Sucos, Eduardo Ribeiro and 24 de Maio. A large choice of Amazonian fruit juices and bar snacks.

$ Sorveteria Glacial, Av Getúlio Vargas 161, and other locations. Recommended for unusual ice creams such as *açaí* and *cupuaçu*.

Tefé *p84*
$$-$ Au Bec d'Or by the port. Simple but very tasty French cuisine using Amazon ingredients.

Leticia (Colombia) *p86*
Plenty of lunchtime estaurants serve cheap dishes of the day in the centre. Fried banana and meat, fish and fruit is sold at the market near the harbour and there are many cheap café/bars overlooking the market on the river bank. Take your own drinking water or beer.
$ Sancho Panza, Cra 10 No 8-72. Good-value meat dishes, big portions, Brazilian beer.

● **Bars and clubs**

Manaus *p75, map p75*
Manaus has lively nightlife with something going on every night. **O Laranjinha** in Ponta Negra is popular any week night and has a live Boi Bumba dance show on Wed.

The scene is constantly changing and clubs and bars are often in different districts far from the centre. The cheapest way of exploring Manaus's nightlife is with a guide.

DJ (Djalma) Oliveira, T092-9112 3942/ 9185 4303, djalmatour@hotmail.com (or book through **Amazon Gero Tours**), will take visitors out to sample Manaus' club life. He is cheaper than a taxi and speaks a little English.

● **Entertainment**

Manaus *p75, map p75*

Cinema
In R 10 de Julho and 8 screens at the **Manaus Plaza Shopping**, Av Djama Batista 2100, www.manausplazashopping.com (3 km from the centre), has the cities best multiplexes. Films are usually dubbed into Portuguese.

Performing arts
For **Teatro Amazonas** and **Centro Cultural Palácio Rio Negro**, see pages 78 and 80. In Praça da Saudade, R Ramos Ferreira, there is sometimes a Sun **funfair** from 1700; try prawns and *calaloo* dipped in *tacaca* sauce.
Teatro da Instalação, R Frei José dos Inocentes 445, T/F092-3234 4096. Performance space in restored historic buildings with free music and dance (from ballet to jazz), May-Dec Mon-Fri at 1800. Charge for Sat-Sun shows. Recommended.

● **Festivals**

Manaus *p75, map p75*
6 Jan Epiphany.
Feb Carnaval in Manaus has spectacular parades in a *sambódromo* modelled on Rio's,

but with 3 times the capacity. Tourists may purchase grandstand seats, but admission at ground level is free (don't take valuables). Carnaval lasts for 5 days, culminating in the parade of the samba schools.

3rd week in Apr A Semana do Indio (Indigenous Brazilian week), a festival celebrating all aspects of indigenous life. Tribal people arrive in Manaus, there are small festivals and events (contact the tourist office for details, see page 77) and indigenous handicrafts are on sale throughout the city.

Jun Festival do Amazonas, a celebration of all the cultural aspects of Amazonas life, indigenous, Portuguese and from the northeast, especially dancing. Also in Jun is the **Festival Marquesiano**, with typical dances from those regions of the world which have sent immigrants to Amazonas, performed by the students of the Colégio Marquês de Santa Cruz.

29 Jun São Pedro, boat processions on the Rio Negro.

Sep Festival de Verão do Parque Dez, 2nd fortnight, festival with music, fashion shows, beauty contests and local foods at the Centro Social Urbano do Parque Dez. In the last week of Sep is the **Festival da Bondade**, with stalls from neighbouring states and countries offering food, handicrafts, music and dancing at SESI, Estr do Aleixo, Km 5.

Oct Festival Universitário de Música (FUM), the most traditional festival of music in Amazonas, organized by the university students, on the university campus.

8 Dec Processão de Nossa Senhora da Conceição, from the Igreja Matriz through the city centre and returning to Igreja Matriz for a solemn Mass.

Parintins *p84*
Jun Festa do Boi Bumba. Huge 3-day festival attracting 40,000 people (see box, page 85).

24 Dec-6 Jan Parintins' other main festival is the Pastorinhas.

São Gabriel da Cachoeira *p87*
Sep Festribal is a very lively indigenous festival in the city. Reachable through **Amazon Gero Tours**.

Shopping

Manaus *p75, map p75*
All shops close at 1400 on Sat and all day Sun. Since Manaus is a free port, the whole area a few blocks off the riverfront is full of electronics shops. This area, known as the **Zona Franca**, is the commercial centre, where the shops, banks and hotels are concentrated.

Markets and souvenirs
To buy a hammock head to the **Casa das Redes** and other shops on R dos Andradas. There are now many handicrafts shops in the area around the theatre. The souvenir shop at the **INPA** (see page 80) has some interesting Amazonian products on sale. The markets near the docks are best in the early morning. There is a very good Sun market in the **Praça do Congresso**, Av E Ribeiro. **Ponta Negra** beach boasts a small 'hippy' market, very lively at weekends. There is a good supermarket at the corner of Av Joaquim Nabuco and R Sete de Setembro.

Central de Artesanato Branco e Silva, R Recife 1999, T092-3642 5458. A gallery of arts and crafts shops and artist's studios selling everything from indigenous art to wooden carvings by renowned Manaus sculptor Joe Alcantara.

Ecoshop, Largo de São Sebastião, T092-3234 8870 and Amazonas Shopping, T092-3642 2026 www.ecoshop.com.br. Indigenous arts and crafts from all over the Amazon, including Yanomami and Tikuna baskets, Wai Wai necklaces and Baniwa palm work.

Galeria Amazonica, R Costa Azevedo 272, Largo do Teatro, T092-3233 4521, www.galeriaamazonica.org.br. A large, modern space filled with Waimiri Atroari indigenous arts and crafts, from weapons, basketware, jewellery and clothing. One of the best places for buying indigenous art in Brazil.

⛰ What to do

Manaus *p75, map p75*

Swimming
Swimming is possible at **Ponta Negra** beach, 13 km from the centre (Soltur bus, US$0.70), although the beach virtually disappears beneath the water Apr-Aug.

There is good swimming at waterfalls on the Rio Tarumã, where there is lunch and shade; crowded at weekends. Take the Tarumã bus from R Tamandaré or R Frei J dos Inocentes, 30 mins, US$0.70 (very few Mon-Fri), getting off at the police checkpoint on the road to Itacoatiara. There is also superb swimming in the natural pools and under falls of clear water in the little streams which rush through the woods, but take locals' advice on swimming in the river; electric eels and various other kinds of unpleasant fish, apart from the notorious piranhas, abound, and industrial pollution of the river is growing.

Every Sun, boats depart from the port in front of the market for beaches along **Rio Negro**, US$2, leaving when full and returning at the end of the day. This is a real locals' day out, with loud music and foodstalls on the sand.

Amazon tours
When booked ahead, agencies listed here will meet visitors at the airport, book Manaus hotels and organize all transfers.

Águia Amazomas Turismo, R 24 de Maio 440 CA-H sala 1, Vila Baipendi, T092-3231 1449, www.aguiaamazonas.com.br. Bespoke trips, lodge stays and cruises conducted by Samuel Basilio – an experienced guide from the upper Rio Negro specializing in long expeditions (who has worked on many BBC documentaries as a location finder), and his brother-in-law Antonio João da Silva.

Amazon Antonio Jungle Tours, c/o Hostel Manaus, R Lauro Cavalcante 231, T092-3234 1294, www.antonio- jungletours.com. Jungle stays on the Rio Urubu, a blackwater river 200 km northeast of Manaus and some of the best-value packages for backpackers and a reliable, well-run service with local, English-speaking guides.

Amazon Explorers, Av Djalma Batista 2100, T092-2133 4777, www.amazonexplorers. com.br. Day tours including the 'meeting of the waters', Lago do Janauari, rubber collecting and lunch a number of lodges (all listed on the website) and booking and transfers for Mamirauá and the Boi Bumba and Parintins. From around US$150 per person per day.

Amazon Gero Tours, R 10 de Julho 695, T092-3232 4755 or T092-9983 6273, www.amazongerotours.com. Excellent tours to a series of lodges around Lago Mamori, transfers to São Gabriel for the festivals, day trips to Presidente Figueiredo and around the city of Manaus (including 'meeting of the waters'), and bookings made for lodges everywhere. Gero, the owner, is very friendly and dedicated and one of the few operators in Manaus genuinely to contribute shares of his profits to the local riverine communities. They also run a lodge at Ararinha lake.

Iguana Tour, R 10 de Julho 679 (hotel 10 de Julho), T092-3663 6507, www.amazon brasil.com.br. Offers an extensive range of trips of various lengths. Good facilities including riverboat, Juma lodge and campsite in the forest.

Manati Amazonia, Av Getúlio Vargas 334, sala 6 at Huascar Figueiredo, T092-3234 2534, www.manatiamazonia.com. A Franco-Brazilian company offering excursions to the Anavilhanas, riverboat cruises and tours in the forests around Mamori with accommodation at **Juma** lodge.

Viverde, R das Guariúbas 47, Parque Acariquar, T092-3248 9988, www.viverde. com.br. A family-run agency acting as a broker for a broad range of Amazon cruises and lodges (including the beautiful **Aldeia dos Lagos** lodge in Silves) and running their own city tours and local excursions.

Amazon cruises
Amazon Clipper, T092-3656 1246, www.amazonclipper.com.br. The leading small boat cruise operator. Excellent trips along the Rio Negro with knowledgeable wildlife guides, including wildlife cruises, sports fishing and bespoke tours. Accommodation is in comfortable cabins, the best of which are private, with en suites and work desks. Set departure dates are listed on the company website. From US$180 per person per day.

Iberostar Grand Amazon, www.iberostar.com.br/amazon/. This leviathan cruises the Amazon (Solimões) river from Manaus on 3 or 4 night trips. With a pool, dance hall, piped music, vast sundeck and space for 200+ people this is hardly an intimate rainforest experience. Each day is peppered with 3 or 4 optional forest and creek excursions on smaller launches. These are often fairly crowded. Those who are environmentally concerned might like to enquire about waste management and the treatment of cruise ship's sewage before booking a trip.

Mamori Community Houseboat tours, through Geraldo Mesquita, T092-3232 4755, geroexpeditions@hotmail.com. River tours on traditional wooden Amazon river boats – some of which are over 40 years old – with accommodation in cabins or hammocks on board and the option of nights camping in the rainforest or spent in traditional riverine communities. Proceeds from the trips revert to the local people. Great value and fascinating.

Guides
Guides sometimes work individually as well as for tour agencies, and the best ones will normally be booked up in advance. Some will only accompany longer expeditions and often subcontract shorter trips. The easiest way to find a guide, however, is through an agency. Advance notice and a minimum of 3 people for all trips is required by the following guides, who are among the best in the city. All can organize bespoke trips (given notice) and can reserve hotels and jungle lodges.

Cristina de Assis, T092-9114 2556, amazonflower@bol.com.br. Cultural city tours telling the story of the city and the rubber boom with visits to the historic buildings and the Museu Seringal. Also trips to the Rio Negro to swim with pink dolphins (these need to be organized at least a week in advance), to the waterfalls at Presidente Figueiredo, the Boi Bumba party in Parintins and the forest. Cristina speaks excellent English and has worked with the Waimiri-Artroari indigenous people.

Matthias Raymond, T092-8115 5716, raymathias@hotmail.com. A Waipixana indigenous guide offering trips to further reaches of the forest including the Pico da Neblina (book in advance). Many languages.

Pedro Neto, T092-8831 1011, pedroffneto@hotmail.com. An adventure tour specialist offering light adventure trips to the large INPA rainforest reserve, the forest around Manaus and the waterfalls and rivers of Presidente Figueiredo – where there is trail-walking, abseiling and birdwatching for spectaculars such as The Guianan Cock of the Rock. Light-hearted but erudite and resolutely great company.

Leticia (Colombia) *p86*
Amazon Jungle Trips, Av Internacional, 6-25, T9819-27377. Lodge-based tours offering a variety of adventure options.
Anaconda Tours, Hotel Anaconda, T9819-27119. Tours to Amacayacu, Isla de los Micos and **Sacambu Lodge**.
Elvis Cuevas, Av Internacional, 6-06, T0819- 27780. An independent guide

offering trips to Amacayacu and indigenous communities nearby.

⊙ Transport

Routes in Amazônia

Belém–Manaus Via **Breves**, **Almeirim**, **Prainha**, **Monte Alegre**, **Curua-Uná**, **Santarém**, **Alenquer**, **Óbidos**, **Juruti** and **Parintins** on the lower Amazon. 5 days upriver, 4 days downriver, including an 18-hr stop in Santarém, suite US$350 upriver, US$250 down, double berth US$180 upriver, US$150 down, hammock space US$75 upriver, US$65 down. Vehicles: small car US$250, *combi* US$320 usually including driver, other passengers extra, 4WD US$450 with 2 passengers, motorcycle US$80. *Nélio Correa* is best on this route. *Defard Vieira*, very good and clean, US$75. *São Francisco* is largest, new and modern, but toilets smelly. *Cisne Branco* of similar quality. *Cidade de Bairreirinha* is the newest on the route, a/c berths. *Lider II* has good food and pleasant atmosphere. *Santarém* is clean, well organized and recommended. *João Pessoa Lopes* is also recommended. The Belém–Manaus route is very busy. Try to get a cabin if you can.

Belém–Santarém Same intermediate stops as above. 2½ days upriver, 1½ days downriver, suite US$150, berth US$135, hammock US$45 upriver, US$38 down. All vessels sailing Belém–Manaus will call at Santarém.

Belém–Macapá (Porto Santana) Non-stop, 8 hrs on fast catamaran, **Atlântica**, US$30, 3 days a week, or 24 hrs on large ships, double berth US$110, hammock space US$30 per person, meals not included but can be purchased onboard (expensive), vehicle US$90, driver not included. *Silja e Souza* (Wed) is best. *Comandante Solon* (Sat) is state run, slightly cheaper, crowded and not as nice. Same voyage via Breves, 36-48 hrs on

smaller riverboats, hammock space US$25 per person including meals. *ENAL* (Sat); *Macamazônia* (every day except Thu), slower and more basic; *Bartolomeu I* of Enavi, food and sanitary conditions OK, 30 hrs; *Rodrigues Alves* has been recommended. *Golfinho do Mar* is said to be the fastest.

Macapá (Porto Santana)–Santarém Via **Vida Nova**, **Boca do Jari**, **Almeirim**, **Prainha**, and **Monte Alegre** on the lower Amazon (does not call at Belém). 2 days upriver, 1½ days downriver, berth US$130, hammock US$40. Boats include *Viageiro V* (nice) and *São Francisco de Paula*.

Santarém–Itaituba Along the Rio Tapajós, 24 hrs (bus service on this route is making the river trip less common).

Manaus-Parintins-Santarém Same intermediate stops as above. 2 days upriver, 1½ days downriver, fares berth US$85, hammock US$30. All vessels sailing Belém–Manaus will call in Santarém and there are others operating only the Santarém–Manaus route, including: *Cidade de Terezinha III* and *IV*, good. *Miranda Dias*, family-run and friendly. Speedboats (*lanchas*) are sometimes available on this route, 16 hrs sitting, no hammock space, US$35. **Ajato** fast boats run Manaus–Parintins (**Pérola**, Thu-Fri, 7 hrs, US$90, **Princesa Lana**, Wed, 6 hrs, US$90).

Manaus–Porto Velho Via **Borba**, **Manicoré** and **Humaitá** on the Rio Madeira. 4 days upriver, 3½ days downriver (up to 7 days when the river is low), double berth US$280, hammock space US$85 per person.

Manaus–Tefé Via **Codajás** and **Coari**, 24-36 hrs, double berth US$70, 1st-class hammock space US$20 per person. *Capitão Nunes* is good. *Jean Filho* also okay. Note that it is difficult to continue west from Tefé to

Tabatinga without first returning to Manaus. **Ajato** fast boats run Manaus–Tefé (**A Jato 2001**, Wed and Sat, 7 hrs, US$85.

Manaus–Tabatinga Via **Fonte Boa**, **Foz do Mamaria**, **Tonantins**, **Santo Antônio do Içá**, **Amataura**, **Monte Cristo**, **São Paulo de Olivença** and **Benjamin Constant** along the Rio Solimões. Up to 8 days upriver (depending on cargo), 3 days downriver, double berth US$280, hammock space US$65 per person (can be cheaper downriver). When going from Peru into Brazil, there is a thorough police check some 5 hrs into Brazil. *Voyagers, Voyagers II* and *III* recommended; *Almirante Monteiro, Avelino Leal* and *Capitão Nunes VIII* all acceptable; *Dom Manoel*, cheaper, acceptable but overcrowded. **Ajato** fast boats run Manaus–Tabatinga (AJato 2000, Tue, 30 hrs, US$150).

Manaus–São Gabriel da Cachoeira Via **Novo Airão**, **Moura**, **Carvoeiro**, **Barcelos** and **Santa Isabel do Rio Negro** along the Rio Negro. Berth US$180, hammock US$60, most locals prefer to travel by road. Boats on this route: *Almirante Martins I* and *II*, *Capricho de Deus, Manoel Rodrigues, Tanaka Netto* departing from São Raimundo dock, north of main port.

Manaus *p75, map p75*

Air

Taxi fare to airport US$17.50, fixed rate, or take bus marked 'Aeroporto Internacional' from Marquês de Santa Cruz at Praça Adalberto Vale, near the cathedral, US$1, or from Ed Garagem on Av Getúlio Vargas every 30 mins. No buses 2200-0700. It is sometimes possible to use the more regular, faster service run by the **Hotel Tropical**; many tour agencies offer free transfers without obligation. Check all connections on arrival. Allow plenty of time at Manaus airport,

formalities are very slow especially if you have purchased duty-free goods.

Many flights depart in the middle of the night and while there are many snack bars there is nowhere to rest. Local flights leave from Terminal 2. Check in advance which terminal you leave from.

There are international flights to **Panama City**, **Miami** and **Atlanta**. For the **Guianas**, a connection must be made in Boa Vista. Domestic flights to **Belém**, **Boa Vista**, **Brasília**, **Cruzeiro do Sul**, **Macapá**, **Parantins**, **Porto Velho**, **Rio Branco**, **Rio de Janeiro**, **Santarém**, **São Paulo**, **Tabatinga**, **Tefé** and **Trombetas**.

Make reservations as early as possible; flights get booked up quickly.

Boat

See Arriving in Manaus, page 76, and Routes in Amazônia, above.

Bus

To get to the *rodoviária* take a local bus from the centre, US$0.70, marked 'Aeroporto Internacional' or 'Cidade Nova' (or taxi, US$5). There are many daily services to **Boa Vista** on **Eucatur**; the best are at night leaving at 2030 and 2100 (10 hrs, US$28). Most go via **Presidente Figueiredo** (3 hrs, US$10). There are also 8 daily buses to **Itacoatiara** (4 hrs, US$15).

Other towns in the state are best visited by air or boat, especially during the Nov to May wet season when road travel is next to impossible.

Car

The road north from Manaus to **Boa Vista** (770 km) is described on page 101. The Catire Highway (BR-319), from Manaus to **Porto Velho** (868 km), has been officially closed since 1990 but is ostensibly set to re-open by 2014. Several bridges are out and there is no repair in sight. The alternative for drivers is to ship a car down river on a barge, others have to travel by boat (see above). To **Itacoatiara**, 285 km east on the Amazon; now paved route AM-010, 266 km, through Rio Preto da Eva.

There are car hire agencies in the airport, including major international companies such as **Localiza** and **Hertz**.

Parintins *p84*

Air
A taxi or motortaxi to the airport costs US$5. Flights to **Manaus** (1¼ hrs), **Belém**, **Santarém** (1 hr 20 mins) with **Trip**, www.voe trip.com.br and **TRIP**, www.trip.com.br.

Boat
Boats call on the Belém–Manaus route: 60 hrs to **Belém** (depending on boat and if going up or down river), 10-26 passengers. There are irregular sailings to **Óbidos** (ask at the port), 12-15 hrs. A boat to **Santarém** takes 20 hrs.

Tefé *p84*

Air
The airport has a connection to **Manaus** with **Trip**, 3 times a week.

Boat
If travelling on to **Tabatinga**, note that Manaus–Tabatinga boats do not usually stop at Tefé. You must hire a canoe to take you out to the main channel and try to flag down the approaching ship.

Benjamin Constant *p85*

Boat
Boats to **Iquitos** leave from a mudbank called **Islandia**, on the Peruvian side of a narrow creek, a few metres from Benjamin Constant. The journey takes a minimum of 2 days upstream, 8-36 hrs downstream, depending on the speed of the boat. On ordinary boats, fares range from US$30-40 per person,

depending on standard of accommodation, food extra. Speedboats charge US$75 per person, three a week are run by **Amazon Tours and Cruises**. All boats call at Santa Rosa (2-3 days upstream to Iquitos were immigration formalities are carried out).

Tabatinga *p86*

Air
The airport has a connection to **Manaus** with **Trip**, 3 times a week.

Boat
Amazon Tours and Cruises operates a luxury service between **Iquitos** and Tabatinga leaving Sun, returning from Tabatinga on Wed, US$695 per person in the Río Amazonas. Also *Arca* US$495 per person, return journey Wed-Sat.

Leticia (Colombia) *p86*

Air
Expect to be searched before leaving Leticia airport, and on arrival in Bogotá from Leticia. **Trip** fly to **Manaus** (sporadically via **Tefé**). There are onward flights from Leticia to **Bogota**.

○ Directory

Manaus *p75, map p75*
Banks Banco do Brasil, Guia Moreira, and airport changes US$ cash, 8% commission, both with ATMs for Visa, Cirrus, MasterCard and Plus. Most offices shut at 1500; foreign exchange operations 0900-1200 only, or even as early as 1100. **Bradesco**, Av 7 de Setembro 895/293, for Visa ATM. **Credicard**, Av Getúlio Vargas 222 for **Diner**'s cash advances. Cash at main hotels; **Câmbio Cortez**, 7 de Setembro 1199, converts TCs into US$ cash, good rates, no commission. **HSBC**, R Dr Moreira 226, ATM for Visa, Cirrus, MasterCard and Plus. Do not change money on the streets. **Embassies and consulates** Most open in the morning

only. **Bolivia**, Av Efigênio Sales 2226, Qd B No 20, T092-3236 9988. **Colombia**, R 24 de Maio 220, Rio Negro Centre, T092-3234 6777, check whether a Colombian tourist card can be obtained at the border. **France**, Av Joaquim Nabuco 1846, T092-3234 2947. **Germany**, R 24 Maio 220, Rio Negro Centre, sala 812, T092-3234 9045, 1000-1200. **Italy**, R Belo Horizonte 240, Adrianópolis, T092-3611 4877. **Japan**, R Fortaleza 460, T092-3232 2000. **Netherlands**, R Miranda Leão 41, T092-3622 1366. **Peru**, R A, casa 1, Conj Aristocrático, Chapada, T092-3236 3012. **Portugal**, R Terezina 193, T092-3234 5777. **Spain**, Al Cosme Ferreira 1225, Aleixo, T092-3644 3800. **UK**, R Paraquê 240, T092-3237 7869. **USA**, R Recife 1010, Adrianópolis, T092-3633 4907, will supply letters of introduction for US citizens. **Venezuela**, R Ferreira Pena 179, T092-3233 6004 (0800-1200), everyone entering Venezuela overland needs a visa. The requirements are 1 passport photo, an onward ticket and the fee, usually US$30 (check in advance for changes to these regulations – it is reported that a yellow fever certificate is not needed). Takes 24 hrs.

Immigration To extend or replace a Brazilian visa, take bus from Praça Adalberto Vale to Kissia Dom Pedro for Polícia Federal post; people in shorts not admitted.

Internet Many around the Teatro, including **Loginet**, R 10 de Julho 625. **Amazon Cyber Cafe**, Av Getúlio Vargas, 626, corner with R 10 de Julho, US$1.50 per hr. **Discover Internet**, R Marcílio Dias 304, next to Praça da Polícia, cabins in back of shop with internet phones and scanners, US$1.50 per hr. Free internet access is available from all public libraries in city, eg **Biblioteca Arthur Reis**, Av 7 de Setembro 444, open 0800-1200 and 1400-1700, with virtual Amazon library and English books. **Laundry Lavanderia Amazonas**, Costa Azevedo 63, near Teatro Amazonas, US$0.40 per item, closed Sat afternoon and Sun. **Lavanderia Central**, R Quintino Bocaiúva

602. **Lavalux**, R Mundurucus 77, fast service washes. **Lavlev**, Av Sen A Maia 1108. One of few self-service laundries is opposite the cemetery, open Sun, a taxi ride away.

Medical services Clínica Sao Lucas, R Alexandre Amorin 470, T092-3622 3678, reasonably priced, some English spoken, good service, take a taxi. **Hospital Tropical**, Av Pedro Teixeira (D Pedro I) 25, T092-3656 1441. Centre for tropical medicine, not for general complaints, treatment free, some doctors speak a little English. Take bus Nos 201 or 214 from Av 7 de Setembro in the city centre. **Pronto Soccoro 28 de Agosto**, R Recife, free for emergencies. **Post office** Main office including poste restante on Mcal Deodoro. On the 1st floor is the philatelic counter where stamps are sold, avoiding the long queues downstairs. Staff don't speak English but are used to dealing with tourists. For airfreight and shipping, **Alfândega**, Av Marquês Santa Cruz (corner of Marechal Deodoro), sala 106. For airfreight and sea mail, **Correio Internacional**, R Monsenhor Coutinho and Av Eduardo Ribeiro (bring your own packaging). **UPS**, T092-3232 9849 (Custódio). **Telephone** International calls can be made from call boxes with a phone card. Also at **Telemar**, Av Getúlio Vargas 950.

Tabatinga *p86*
Banks There is a **Banco do Brasil**, Av da Amizade, which changes TCs at a poor rate and has a Visa ATM. It is easier to get Peruvian money for reais in Leticia. **Internet Infocenter**, Av Amizade 1581.

Leticia (Colombia) *p86*
Banks Banco de Bogotá, will cash Tcs, has ATM on Cirrus network, good rates for Brazilian reais. **Banco Ganadero**, Cra 11, has a Visa ATM. There are street money changers, plenty of *câmbios*, and banks for exchange. Shop around. **Post office** Avianca office, Cra 11 No 7-58. **Telephone** Cra 11/C 9, near Parque Santander.

Roraima

This extreme northern state is one of the country's newest and is only just beginning to exploit its strategic position on the border with Gran Sabana in Venezuela and the stunning Parakaima mountains in Guyana. The state capital is Boa Vista, a safe, tidy modern city with a very lively out-of-season carnival. Beyond the city, the rainforest gives way to extensive grasslands overlooked by precipitous table-top mountains. The most famous of these is Conan Doyle's lost world, Roraima, which can be visited from Boa Vista. Others, such as Tepequen and those on the upper Rio Branco, are more remote and less visited, their wildernesses replete with wildlife. Guyana and Venezuela are a couple of hours from Boa Vista and all visa formalities can be sorted out in that city. Contrary to popular belief, crossing into both countries is easy and painless and there are excellent onward transport services to Caracas or Georgetown. ➤➤ *For listings, see pages 103-105.*

Background

Roraima covers an area nearly twice the size of England but supports a population of just 325,000. Land grants in the 1970s to encourage agricultural development resulted in a rapid increase in population (from only 25,000 in 1960). Then, in the late 1980s a gold rush in the northwest of Roraima drew prospectors from all over the country. The mining took place on the indigenous Yanomami reserve, devastating their traditional way of life. Further tragedy came in January 1998 when forest fires spread across the state, causing massive destruction. The forest cover gives way to grasslands in the northeast and there is a pronounced dry season. The *várzea* (flood plain) along the main rivers irrigates the southeast of the state. Cattle ranching is important as is rice cultivation on the flood plain of the Rio Branco. Other crops are maize, beans, manioc and banana. Some mining continues but at a reduced level.

Towards Boa Vista

The road that connects Manaus and Boa Vista (a ferry crosses the Rio Branco at Caracaraí) is fully paved and regularly maintained. There are service stations with toilets and camping sites every 150-180 km; all petrol is low octane. At Km 117 is **Presidente Figueiredo**, with many waterfalls and a famous cave with bats. There are also shops and a restaurant. About 100 km further on is a service station at the entrance to the **Uaimiri Atroari Indian Reserve**, which straddles the road for about 120 km. Private cars and trucks are not allowed to enter the reserve between sunset and sunrise, but buses are exempt from this regulation. Nobody is allowed to stop within the reserve at any time. At the northern entrance to the reserve there are toilets and a place to hang your hammock (usually crowded with truckers overnight). At Km 327 is the village of **Vila Colina** where **Restaurante Paulista** is clean with good food, and you can use the shower and hang your hammock. At Km 359 there is a monument to mark the **equator**. At Km 434 is the clean and pleasant **Restaurant Goaio**. Just south of Km 500 is **Bar Restaurante D'Jonas**, a good place to eat; you can also camp or sling a hammock. Beyond here, large tracts of forest have been destroyed for settlement, but already many homes have been abandoned.

Boa Vista → *For listings, see pages 103-105. Phone code: 095. Population: 200,000.*

The capital of the extreme northern state of Roraima, 759 km north of Manaus, is a very pleasant, clean, laid-back little town on the Rio Branco. Tourism is beginning here and there are a number of interesting new destinations offering a chance to explore far wilder country than that around Manaus, with correspondingly richer wildlife. The landscape is more diverse, too, with tropical forest, savannah and highlands dotted with waterfalls. However, the area immediately around the city has been heavily deforested.

Boa Vista lies within easy access of both Venezuela and Guyana and crossing the border to either is straightforward. When the river is low, it is possible to swim in the Rio Branco, 15 minutes by bus from the town centre (too polluted in Boa Vista). As a result of heavy international pressure, the Brazilian government expelled some 40,000 gold prospectors from the Yanomami Reserve in the west of the state in the early 1990s. The economic consequences were very severe for Boa Vista, which went from boom to bust. An increase in cattle ranching in the area has not taken up the slack.

Arriving in Boa Vista

The **airport** ① *4 km from the centre*, receives national and international flights. There are no exchange or left luggage facilities. A taxi to the centre costs US$20; to the *rodoviária*, US$10. There is a bus to the centre, US$1, or a 45-minute walk.

The **rodoviária** ① *Av das Guianas, 3 km out of town at the end of Av Ville Roy, T095-3224 0606*, receives several daily buses from Manaus, Bonfim (from the Guyanese border) and Santa Elena in Venezuela. A taxi to the centre costs US$5, or the 10-minute bus ride costs US$0.45. The local bus terminal is on Avenida Amazonas, by Rua Cecília Brasil, near the central *praça*.

The city has a modern, functional plan, which often means long, hot treks from one place to another. The rather ineffectual state tourism office **Detur** ① *R Coronel Pinto 267, Centro, Boa Vista, T095-2121 2525, www.turismo.rr.gov.br*, also has booths at the *rodoviária*, T095-3623 1238, and the airport. ➤➤ *See Transport, page 104.*

Boa Vista

Where to stay
Aipana Plaza **1**
Barrudada Palace **5**
Euzébio's **2**
Ideal **4**
Uiramutam Palace **3**

Restaurants
Churrascaria La Carreta **4**
1000 Sabores **1**
Frangão **2**
Peixada Tropical **3**

To Venezuela and Guyana → *For listings, see pages 103-105.*

Boa Vista has road connections with the Venezuelan frontier at **Santa Elena de Uairén**, 237 km away. The road is paved, but the only petrol available is 110 km south of Santa Elena. Boa Vista is also linked to Bonfim for the Guyanese border at **Lethem**. Both roads are open all year.

Santa Elena de Uairén (Venezuela) → *International phone code +58.*

Santa Elena de Uairén is the gateway to the Venezuelan Highlands for those entering the country from Brazil. It is a pleasant frontier town, 10-12 hours by bus from Ciudad Bolívar, which is nine hours from Caracas. The road is paved all the way and there are also flights. The landscape is beautiful, an ancient land of flat-topped mountains and waterfalls. The road skirts the **Parque Nacional Canaima**, which boasts the highest waterfall in the world, the **Angel Falls** (Salto Angel). Not far north of Santa Elena is the route to Mount Roraima.

Santa Elena has plenty of hotels and places to eat, as well as money-changing facilities, a phone office with international connections, and tour companies for trips into the Gran Sabana – as the region is known.

Arriving in Santa Elena de Uairén The **rodoviária** ⓘ *C Mcal Sucre*, receives arrivals from Ciudad Bolívar (Venezuela) several times daily; the journey takes 10-12 hours and buses are run by a number of companies. There are plenty of accommodation options in Santa Elena de Uairén, but just one basic hotel on the Brazilian side of the border. ▶▶ *See Transport, page 105.*

Lethem (Guyana)

A small but scattered town on the Brazilian border (see below), this is the service centre for the Rupununi and for trade with Brazil. There are many small stores, a small hospital (T772 2006), a police station (T772 2011) and government offices. A big event at Easter is the rodeo, visited by cowboys from all over the Rupununi. Prices are about twice as high as in Georgetown. About 2.5 km south of town at St Ignatius there is a Jesuit mission dating from 1911. In the nearby mountains there is good birdwatching and there are waterfalls to visit.

There is another border crossing at **Laramonta** from where it is a hard but rewarding walk to the Guyanese town of Orinduik.

Roraima listings

For hotel and restaurant price codes and other relevant information, see pages 10-13.

⬤ Where to stay

Boa Vista *p102, map p102*
$$ Aipana Plaza, Joaquim Nabuco 53, Praça do Centro Cívico, T095-3224 4800, www.aipanaplaza.com.br. The best in town with plain rooms decorated in cream and dark tiles, and photos of Roraima. Hot water, a/c, marble bathrooms and cable TV. Attractive pool area with a shady little bar.
$$ Barrudada Palace Hotel, R Araújo Filho 228, T095-2121 1700, www.hotelbarrudada.tur.br. Simple a/c rooms in a modern tower block with a pool and restaurant, very close to the centre. Rooms on the upper floors have views of the river. Breakfast and lunch included.

$$ Uiramutam Palace, Av Capt Ene Garcez 427, T095-3624 4700, www.uiramutam.com.br. A business hotel with modest a/c rooms with writing desk and armchair, cable TV and large bathrooms. Decent pool.

$ Euzébio's, R Cecília Brasil 1107, T095-2121 0300, www.hoteleuzebios.com.br. Spruce, modest rooms with a/c and en suites with cold showers. The best are airy and on the upper floors. Pleasant pool and a laundry service.

$ Hotel Ideal, R Araújo Filho 533, T095-3224 6342. Very simple but well-kept rooms with en suites. Some have a/c. Friendly staff and generous breakfast. Convenient for the centre.

Camping
Rio Cauamé, 3 km north of town. Pleasant unofficial site with small bar and clean river.

⑦ Restaurants

Boa Vista *p102, map p102*
Most restaurants close at night, except for pizzerias. There are a number of restaurants serving snacks and juices on the riverside along **R Floriano Peixoto** and several open-air restaurants and cafés on the **Orla Taumanan**, a complex of little bars and Restaurants places overlooking the river. Nightlife and bars are concentrated here; it is quiet during the week but livelier at weekends. There are many little juice stands around **Praça do Centro Cívico**.

$$ Churrascaria La Carreta, R Pedro Rodrigues 185, 500 m from **Euzébio's**, T095-3224 0165. With a good-value US$5 buffet, with plenty of choice and a vibrant, friendly atmosphere. Recommended.

$$ Euzébio's (see Where to stay above). Decent fish, *feijoada* and meat dishes. Generous breakfast.

$$ Peixada Tropical, R Pedro Rodrigues at Ajuricaba 1525, T095-3224 6040. River fish dishes in a variety of styles from Bahian

sauces to *milanesa* accompanied by beans, rice and salads.

$ 1000 Sabores, R Araújo Filho at Benjamin Constant. Opens early and closes late. Pizzas, snacks and juices.

$ Frangão, R Homem de Melo at Cecília Brasil 965, T095 3224 8240. Chicken and river fish with salads, rice, beans.

① Bars and clubs

Boa Vista *p102, map p102*
R Floriano Peixoto is lively after dark at weekends when there is live music in and around the Orla Taumanan.

▲ What to do

Boa Vista *p102, map p102*
Aguia Tours, R Benjamin Constant 1683, T095-3624 1516. Can book buses and flights and the owner speaks some English.
Roraima Adventures, R Coronel Pinto 86, sala 106, T095-3624 9611, T095-3623 6972, www.roraima-brasil.com.br. Interesting trips to little-known and little-visited parts of Roraima state, including the spectacular Tepequen and Serra Grande mountains and the Rio Uraricoera, which is replete with wildlife. Also regular expeditions to the Pico da Neblina and Mount Roraima itself. Groups get the best prices, which are competitive with those in Manaus. Helpful with visas for Venezuela, reliable and professional.

⊖ Transport

Boa Vista *p102, map p102*

Air
A taxi to the airport costs US$20. Flights and buses and flights can be booked through **Aguia Tours** or **Roraima Adventures** (see What to do , above).

The airport has flights to the **Guianas**, **Belém**, **Brasília**, **Macapá**, **Manaus**, **Santarém** and **São Paulo**. Confirm flights before reaching Boa Vista as they are often fully booked. Air taxis can be booked with **Rondônia**, Praça Santos Dumond, T095-3224 5068.

 Airline offices **GOL**, www.voe gol.com.br. **META**, Praça Santos Dumont 100, T095-3224 7677, www.voe meta.com.br. **TAM**, www.tam.com.br.

Bus

Note that it is difficult to get a taxi or bus to the *rodoviária* in time for early morning departures; as it's a 25-min walk, book a taxi the previous evening. To **Manaus**, with **Eucatur**, US$35, 10-12 hrs, 4 daily each way, can be crowded, advisable to book at least a few hours in advance. To **Caracaraí** US$12, 3 hrs. **Amatur** to **Bonfim**, daily 0730, 1430, 1700, 2 hrs, US$7.

Car hire

Localiza, Av Benjamin Constant 291E, T/F095-3224 5222. **Yes**, Av Maj Williams 538, T/F095-3224 3723.

Taxis

For radio taxis contact **Tupã**, R Monte Castelo 318, T095-3224 9150.

Border with Venezuela *p103*
Bus Buses from Santa Elena to **Boa Vista** leave at 0830, 1200, 1500 and 1600, stopping at all checkpoints, US$15, 3½-6 hrs, take water. It is possible to share a taxi.

Border with Guyana *p103*

Bus
Bonfim–Boa Vista at least 3 a day, US$7. Weekly jeep **Laramonta–Boa Vista** US$30.

Boat
To cross the river, take a canoe, US$0.25. No boats at night.

Directory

Boa Vista *p102, map p102*
Banks US$ and Guyanese notes can be changed in Boa Vista. TCs and cash in **Banco do Brasil**, Av Galycon de Paiva 56, 1000-1300 (minimum US$200), will not change *bolívares*. There is no official exchange agency and the local rates for bolivares are low. **Bradesco**, Jaime Brasil e Getúlio Vargas, Visa ATM. Best rate for dollars, **Casa Pedro José**, R Araújo Filho 287, T095-3224 4277, also changes TCs and bolivares. **Embassies and consulates** Venezuela, Av Benjamin Constant 968, T095-3623 9285, open mornings only. Visas available. Laid-back service. Allow 24-48 hrs. **Guyana**, there is currently no consular service for Guyana in Roraima, this may change – see www.guyana. org/govt for the latest information. **Medical services** Geral, Av Brig Eduardo Gomes, T095-3623 2068. Free yellow fever inoculations at a clinic near the hospital.

Rondônia and Acre

The state of Rondônia is largely populated by migrants from other parts of Brazil. Foreigners are welcomed without question or curiosity and there is no regional accent. A local academic described the state as 'a land where nobody has a name and everyone can have a dream'. Most visitors tend to arrive via the BR-364 from Cuiabá or the Rio Madeira from Manaus.

The intriguing state of Acre, rich in natural beauty, history and the seringueiro culture, was very much off the beaten track until 2010, when regular bus services and flights connected the state, and its capital city Rio Branco, with Cusco in Peru. Acre is now a viable entry or exit point for Brazil and the state is beginning to develop its considerable potential for adventure, with some of the best indigenous and ecotourism projects in the Amazon region, many of them in very remote country.

Porto Velho → *For listings, see pages 114-117. Phone code: 069. Population: 330,000.*

Porto Velho stands on a high bluff overlooking a curve of the Rio Madeira, one of the Amazon's main tributaries. The city has seen the rubber, gold and timber booms come and go. Service and IT industries are now the major employers. The city is a large sprawl of streets, laid out in blocks stretching 8 km into the interior. The lack of town planning means that many of the best shops, hotels and banks are now a fair distance from the old centre near the river. The city is increasingly prosperous as the result of government money flooding in to fund huge twin hydroelectric dam projects on the Rio Madeira, a few kilometres upstream of the city centre. This is one of the largest civil engineering projects in the world. And whilst the scheme may be of dubious environmental pedigree, it is renovating a once tawdry Porto Velho. Some 80% of the city's sewage is treated, making Porto Velho one of the first Brazilian cities not to pump most of its raw discharge into a river or the sea. Buildings in the centre are being renovated and by 2012 the city will be graced with a very attractive waterfront promenade. That said, there is little in Porto Velho for tourists and very little organized tourism in the Rondônia Amazon, and the only real reason to come here is en route to or from Bolivia or Acre.

Arriving in Porto Velho
Getting there Porto Velho is well connected, with flights on Gol, Avianca, TAM and TRIP to destinations including Cuiabá, Campo Grande, Rio Branco, Manaus, Brasília, São Paulo, Belém and Fortaleza. These arrive at the **Aeroporto Gov Jorge Teixeira De Oliveira** ① *8 km west of town, T069-3225 1755.* A taxi to downtown costs US$25 and 'aeroporto'

buses run every 40 minutes 0700-1900 between the aiport and Rua Carlos Gomes in the city centre. There is a CAT (Centro ao Atendimento Turistico) at the airport – with no English and a few pamphlets. Interstate buses from Rio Branco and Cuiabá arrive at the **rodoviária** ⓘ *east of the centre, Jorge Teixeira, between Carlos Gomes and Dom Pedro II*. There are buses to downtown. ➤➤ *See Transport, page 117.*

Getting around Urban bus services are good. Consider hiring a car if you're going to stay for some time, as the city is very spread out. Be patient as even local residents get confused with directions. Taxis in town are cheap and plentiful. Find your favourite driver and stick with him; all have mobile phones and work with partners to give prompt 24-hour service.

Tourist office CMTUR ⓘ *R Jose do Patrocinio 852, Centro, T069-3901 3186, www.portovelho. ro.gov.br*, is helpful, though staff speak little to no English. The office publishes a glossy pamphlet and is enthusiastic about improvements being made to the city. They can also recommend sports fishing operators and a handful of destinations to visit around the city.

Places in Porto Velho
At the top of the hill on Praça João Nicoletti is the **cathedral**, built in 1930, with beautiful stained-glass windows. The **prefeitura** (town hall) is across the street. The principal commercial street is Avenida 7 de Setembro, which runs from the railway station to the upper level of the city, near the *rodoviária*. The centre is hot and noisy, but not without its charm, and the port and old railway installations with their steam locomotives and crumbling wharves are interesting. The whole area is due to be completely rebuilt in 2012, with a refurbished **Museu Ferroviário** (railway museum – currently closed) and a waterfront park populated with Amazon wildlife and dotted with Amazon-lily-covered ponds. Newly polished steam trains will run once more on a short stretch of the old Rio **Madeira-Mamoré** railway. Brazil was required to construct this railway – between Porto

Porto Velho

Where to stay 🛏
Central 1
Líder 2
Samauma 5
Tia Carmen 4
Vila Rica 3

Restaurants 🍴
Café Madeira 1
Caravela do Madeira 2
Myoshi 3

300 metres
300 yards

Velho and Riberalt in Bolivia – under the 1903 Treaty of Petrópolis, in part exchange for Bolivia's ceding of Acre. The line barely reached Guajará-Mirim, and so many died in its construction that it was said that each 100 sleepers were paid for with a human life. The new tourist section of the railway will only run as far as Porto Velho's suburbs.

The neoclassical **Palácio do Governo** faces Praça Getúlio Vargas, while Praça Marechal Rondon is spacious and modern. There are several popular viewpoints overlooking the river and railway yards. **Mirante I** (with restaurant) is at the end of Rua Carlos Gomes; **Mirante II** (with a bar and ice cream parlour) is at the end of Rua Dom Pedro II and **Mirante III** (with restaurant) is at the end of Benjamin Constant.

It is possible to visit the **cemetery**, where many of the people who died during the construction of the railway are buried. It's about 3 km from the railway station and best to go with a local guide, as it is located in a poorer part of town and difficult to find. It is an eerie place, with many of the tombstones overgrown, some of which have been tampered with by practitioners of *macumba*, and there are rumoured to be ghosts.

Parque Nacional Municipal de Porto Velho ① *Av Rio Madeira s/n, 10 km, T069-221 2769, Thu-Sun, volunteer guides*, is a small zoo with 12 km of marked trails.

Excursions from Porto Velho

The **Banho do Souza** is a bar, restaurant and swimming area, 36 km out of town on the BR-364. A coolbox of beers and soft drinks is left by your table and you pay for what you've drunk at the end of the afternoon, swimming is free.

Along the BR-364 → *For listings, see pages 114-117.*

The **Marechal Rondon Highway**, BR-364, runs 1550 km from Porto Velho to Cuiabá in Mato Grosso. The paving of this road has led to the development of farms and towns. Cattle ranches can be seen all along the road, with the lowest population density in the south between Pimenta Bueno and Vilhena.

Pousada Ecológica Rancho Grande ① *contact Caixa Postal 361, Ariquemes, Rondônia 78914, T/F069-3532 2300, www.ranchogrande.com.br*, is a working *fazenda* about 250 km south of Porto Velho. It contains millions of rare butterflies, about 450 bird species and numerous mammals, all of which can be seen on the 20 km of trails. Owner, Harald Schmitz, speaks English, German and Spanish. Highly recommended, especially for butterfly lovers. Reservations and tours can be arranged through the fazenda's website.

Parque Nacional dos Pacaás Novos protects some 765,800 ha of *cerrado*, rainforest and tropical savannah and lies west of the BR-364. The fauna includes all the spectacular mammals such as jaguar, brocket deer, puma, tapir, peccary and maned wolf. The average annual temperature is 23°C, but this can fall as low as 5°C when the cold front known as the *friagem* blows up from the south pole. Information is available from **Instituto Chico Mendes de Conservação da Biodiversidade (ICMBio)** ① *www.icmbio. gov.br*. There is another large reserve, the **Jaru Biological Reserve** in the east of the state. No tour operators visit either to date.

On the Rio Guaporé, the **Guaporé Biological Reserve** ① *Av Limoeira, CEP 78971, Guaporé, T069-3651 2239*. contains the Forte Príncipe da Beira. The fort was constructed in 1777 to defend the border with Bolivia and is currently being restored. It can be reached from Costa Marques (20 km by road), which is some 345 km by unpaved road west of

Rolim de Moura. This unplanned town, 40 km west of Pimenta Bueno, relies on agriculture, livestock and a small furniture industry. There are a few basic hotels and guesthouses, which are easy to find and do not require reservations.

Guajará-Mirim → *For listings, see pages 114-117. Phone code: 069. Population: 39,000.*

From Porto Velho, the paved BR-364 continues 220 km southwest to **Abunã** (with a few cheap hotels), where the BR-425 branches south to Guajará-Mirim. About 9 km east of Abunã is a ferry crossing over the Rio Madeira, where it receives the waters of the Rio Abunã. The BR-425 is a fair road, partly paved, which uses the former rail bridges. It is sometimes closed from March to May. Across the Mamoré from Guajará-Mirim is the Bolivian town of **Guayaramerín**, which is connected by road to Riberalta, from where there are air services to other Bolivian cities.

Guajará-Mirim is a charming town. The **Museu Municipal** ① *T069-3541 3362, 0500-1200, 1400-1800*, at the old Guajará-Mirim railway station beside the ferry landing, is interesting, diverse, and recommended. An ancient stern wheeler plies the Guaporé. Return trips of 1250 km, taking 26 days, can be made from Guajará-Mirim to Vila Bela in Mato Grosso; the fare includes food.

There are seven buses daily between Porto Velho and Gujará-Mirim, taking three to five hours and one to Rio Branco (10 hours). Speedboats cross the river for Bolivia at least every 30 minutes (when full). There are plenty of money changers on both sides of the river. **Brazilian immigration** is at the Polícia Federal, Avenida Presidente Dutra, 70 Cristo Rei, T069- 3541 2437, 0830-1200 and 1400-1800.

Guayaramerín (Bolivia) → *International phone code +591.*

The Bolivian town of Guayaramerín is a cheerful, prosperous little place, on the bank of the Río Mamoré. It has an important **Zona Libre**. There are flights to Trinidad, La Paz, Cobija, Cochabamba and Santa Cruz, as well as buses to La Paz, Santa Cruz, Trinidad, Cobija and other destinations, but the roads are in poor shape and appalling in the wet season. Boats run upriver to Trinidad. **Bolivian immigration** is at Avenida Costañera at Calle Mariscal Santa Cruz, T(+591) 855 4413, Monday-Friday 0800-1200 and 1400-1800, Saturday 0830-1200.

Acre

In the mid-19th century, what is now Acre was disputed land between Brazil and Bolivia. The Treaty of Ayacucho, 1866, gave the territory to Bolivia. However, the onset of the rubber boom in the 1880s upset this arrangement because many of the landowners who were exporting rubber from Acre and down the Rio Madeira were Brazilian. They resented the fact that the Bolivian government had nominal control, exacting duties, but had signed economic rights over to North American interests. Many *Nordestinos* also migrated to this western frontier at the time in search of fortune. In 1899 the Brazilians rebelled. Four years later the Bolivian government yielded the territory to Brazil under the Treaty of Petrópolis and the American company received US$2 million compensation. In 1913, Rio Branco became capital of the new Território Federal do Acre, which attained statehood in 1962.

Acre has a population of only 500,000 but, as its land is much more productive than that of Rondônia. In the 1990s there was a flood of migration from Acre's landless south into the its neighbouring state, and conditions have yet to be improved. Acre is slightly drier than Rondônia, with 1.5-2 m of rain a year.

Rio Branco → *For listings, see pages 114-117. Phone code: 068. Population: 253,000.*

Remote Rio Branco, 4287 km from Rio, is one of Brazil's surprises. Rather than being the scruffy frontier town of most Brazilians' popular imagination, it's one of the country's neatest, safest (and smallest) state capitals, with manicured public spaces, orderly cycleways and a lively waterfront promenade, the Mercado Velho, which buzzes with bar life in the evenings and at weekends. The city is a pleasant place to stopover en route to the attractions further east – the great forests of Acre and beyond to the Andes, Bolivia and Peru.

The Rio Acre divides Rio Branco into two districts – **Primeiro** (west bank) and **Segundo** (east bank), on either side of the river, linked by two bridges. The central Primeiro district contains most of the sights including the shady main square, **Praça Plácido de Castro**. This is lined with modest buildings of state, including the handsome, neoclassical **Palácio Rio Branco** ① *Av Getúlio Vargas s/n, T068-3223 9240, Wed-Fri 0800-1800, Sat-Sun 1600-2100, free,* looking like a mini-White House and housing a museum devoted to the story of Acre. Nearby, along Avenida Brasil, is the **Nossa Senhora de Nazaré** ① *Av Brasil s/n, T068-3224 1932, Mon-Fri 0800-1800, Sat 0700-1230, Sun 0600-0900 and 1600-2000, www.diocesriobranco.com.br, free,* which is worth a quick visit to see the huge psychedelic murals and stained-glass windows showing the stations of the cross. A large park, the **Parque da Maternidade**, runs through the entire city centre in the *Primeiro* for 6 km, with

Rio Branco

Where to stay 🛏
Afa Hotel & Restaurant 1
Imperador Galvez 3
Irmãos Inácio Palace 2

Loureiro 4
Ouro Verde 5
Papai 6
Terra Verde 7

Restaurants 🍴
Elcio 1
Mata Nativa 2

cycle paths, shady areas and hundreds of hummingbrids flitting through the trees. There are plenty of cafés for a juice or snack and a museum, the **Casa Povos da Floresta** ① *Parque da Maternidade s/n, T068-3224 5667, Wed-Fri 0800-1800, Sat-Sun 1600-2100, free*, devoted to Acre's indigenous peoples and *caboclos*. A small arts and crafts centre nearby, the **Casa de Artesão** ① *Parque da Maternidade s/n, T068-3223 0010, Mon-Sat 0900-2000, free*, sells work by a cooperative of craftsmen from all over Acre.

The city's prettiest streets line the riverbank around the **Mercado Velho** (Rio Acre at Avenida Epaminondas). The latter building was built in the 1920s and was recently refurbished. The streets overflow with cafés, bars and craft shops and it is always busy with people drinking and chatting al fresco in the evenings.

Acre's oldest street, **Rua Eduardo Assmar**, lies on the other side of the river in *Segundo*. It is lined with tiny art deco shops dating from the 1920s. Look out for the old cinema, the **Cine Teatro Recreio**, which must have been one the remotest picture house in the world when it was constructed during the rubber boom.

There are a few other sights. The **Museu da Borracha** ① *Av Ceará 1144, T068-3223 1202, Tue-Fri 0800-1800, Sat-Sun 1600-2100, free*, which tells the story of the Acre rubber trade and the guerrilla war against Bolivia by the Cearenses who came here from Fortaleza – 6500 km away. The **Parque Chico Mendes** ① *Rodovia AC-40, km 07, Vila Acre, T068-3221 1933, Wed-Sun 0700-1700, free*, preserves tropical forests, which are cut with trails and rich with birdlife, a replica of a rubber-tapper settlement, a zoo and a memorial to Chico Mendes who died in nearby Xapuri (see page 112). The **Horto Forestal**, in Vila Ivonete (Primeiro), 3 km north of the centre, is popular with joggers and has native Amazonian trees, a small lake, walking paths and picnic areas (take a city bus to 'Conjunto Procon' or 'Vila Ivonete'). The Brazilian spiritual movement of **Santo Daime**, devoted to taking Ayahuasca (daime) in group sessions, was founded in Rio Branco by Sebastião Mota de Melo, and has numerous churches and facilities in Rio Branco, including the Céu do Mapiá (www.ceudomapia.org), on the outskirts of the city.

The airport on the AC-40, Km 1.2, in the Distrito Segundo, T068-3224 6833, receives flights from several Brazilian cities. A taxi from the airport to the centre costs a flat rate of US$20, or take a bus marked 'Custódio Freire' or 'Terminal Urbano', US$0.90. Buses arrive at the **rodoviária** ① *Av Uirapuru, Cidade Nova, Segundo distrito, T069-3224 1182*. To get to the centre, take a city bus marked 'Norte–Sul'. For tourist information, contact the Secretaria de Indústria e Comércio ① *Av Getúlio Vargas 659, Centro*, or the Departamento de Turismo ① *BR-364, Km 5, Distrito Industrial, T068-3224 3997*.

The **Aeroporto Internacional de Rio Branco-Plácido de Castro** ① *Estrada BR- 364 km 18, Sena Madureira, T068-3211 1003*, is just under 10 km from the city centre. Taxis cost US$15, or take any bus marked 'Custódio Freire' (US$1) to the urban bus terminal in the city centre. Buses also run from here to the *rodoviária*, 5 km from the city centre at Avenida Uirapuru, Cidade Nova, Distrito Segundo, T068-3224 6984. The **Secretária de Turismo** (SETUL) ① *at the Estádio (football stadium), Av Chico Mendes, T068-3201 3024, Mon-Fri 1000-1800, Sat 1200-1700, www.ac.gov.br*. There is a **CAT office** ① *Praça Povos da Floresta (Praça Eurico Dutra), T068-3901 3029, Mon-Sat 0900-1800*.

Excursions from Rio Branco

About 8 km southeast of town, upriver on the Rio Acre, is **Lago do Amapá**, a U-shaped lake good for boating and water sports; access is by river or by land via route AC-40. About

2 km beyond along the AC-40 is **Praia do Amapá**, a bathing beach on the Rio Acre; an annual arts festival is held here in September. Excursions can be made to **rubber plantations** and rubber extraction areas in native forest (*seringais nativos*).

Some 13 km from Rio Branco is **Colônia Cinco Mill** (access along AC-10), a religious centre of the followers of the Santo Daime doctrine. Its members, many originally from outside Acre and Brazil, live a communal life, working in agriculture and producing crafts made of latex. The religion centres around the use of *ayahuasca*, a hallucinogenic potion. Visitors are usually welcome, but enquire beforehand.

Cruzeiro do Sul and around

From Rio Branco, the BR-364 continues west to Cruzeiro do Sul, Japim and the Peruvian frontier, running through cleared ground around the capital but quickly entering towering forest, which continues to the snaking rivers and jagged mountains of the **Serra do Divisor** in Acre and Brazil's far western frontier. This is pioneer country for tourism, wild in the main and with large numbers of indigenous Brazilians, especially in the forests of the **Vale do Juruá**. One of the best tour operators in the Amazon, **Maanaim Amazônia** (see page 116) run visits here several times a year.

Cruzeiro do Sul itself feels about as isolated as a medium-sized town can feel. Amazonas state, whose border is just north of town, stretches in unbroken trees for more than 1000 km before reaching the tiny outpost of Benjamin Constant; itself unreachable by road; and it's a similar story to the south and the west. Cruzeiro is a sleepy place. Cheap excursions can be made on the river, for example to the village of **Rodrigues Alves**, two to three hours' return by boat or 15 km by road. In the jungle it's possible to see rubber tapping and the collecting of latex in *borrachas*. It's difficult to change money in Cruzeiro do Sul.

The BR-364 is unpaved and a single bus a day makes the 672-km journey between Rio Branco taking anything from 14 to 20 hours, depending on conditions. There are daily flights. The road is frequently impassable and open, on average, around 20 days a year. Flights connect the town with Rio Branco (**Gol & Trip**) and Pucallpa in Peru. In the wet season there are sporadic boats to Manaus (seven to 10 days). There are a few basic, boxy hotels in town (near the cathedral and facing the river), many offer fullboard. West of Cruzeiro do Sul the Amazonian forests stretch to one of the world's remotest and largest national parks, the 843,000-ha **Parque Nacional da Serra do Divisor**. It is made up of a series of ancient, craggy table-top mountains dripping with waterfalls which mark a transition between the Amazon lowlands and the foothills of the Andes. The park has been little studied, but according to the Instituto Chico Mendes de Conservação da Biodiversidade it has one of the highest levels of biodiversity in the Brazilian Amazon. Visits can be made with **Maanaim** (see page 116).

Xapuri

Chico Mendes' home town is little more than a few houses and shops straddling the BR-317, which runs from Rio Branco to Assis Brasil and Brasiléia on the borders of Peru and Bolivia. But it's well worth stopping for a day or two. Chico's house is one of two buildings preserved as a small cultural centre and museum, the **Fundação Chico Mendes** ① *T068-3542 2651, Mon-Sat 0900-1700, US$3*. The main building showcases memorabilia associated with the environmentalist, including prizes and awards given by international and Brazilian bodies, photographs and letters. His very simple wooden house is preserved as it was when Chico

Chico Mendes – eco-martyr

The most famous *seringueiro* (rubber tapper) was Francisco (Chico) Alves Mendes, born in 1944. Chico's father had come to Acre from northeast Brazil as a *soldado da borracha*, engaged in providing rubber for the Allies during the Second World War. Chico learnt the trade of his father, became a leader of the Xapuri Rural Workers' Union and was a founder member of the CNS. He was instrumental in setting up a number of extractive reserves, parcels of land preserved for sustainable exploitation by those that lived there. He was shot dead on 22 December 1988 by cattle ranchers, to whose land-grabbing Mendes was in open opposition. He was by no means the only *seringueiro* who had been killed in such circumstances (he was the 90th rubber tapper to be killed in 1988 alone), but his murder was the culmination of a decade of *fazendeiro-seringueiro* confrontation. Over 4000 people attended his funeral; the world's media latched onto the story and Chico Mendes became the first globally-recognized eco-martyr. He was honoured by the United Nations for his efforts to stop the destruction of the rainforest. The universal outcry at his assassination led to the arrest, trial and imprisonment of his killers, members of the family of Darly Alves da Silva; a rare event in the history of Amazon land disputes. His death inspired changes in government policy on environmental protection, greater involvement of rubber tappers and other forest workers in local organizations, and the development of extractive reserves, first promoted in 1985 as protected areas for the *seringueiros*. Father Andre Ficarelli, assistant to the Bishop of Acre, said that Mendes' murder was like "the lancing of a tumour, exposing all the corruption and problems which the government [chose] to ignore". To others it was an opportunity to portray the whole affair in Hollywood-style melodrama; there was fierce competition for the film rights to Mendes' life story.

But Chico has left a lasting legacy. The forests he fought to preserve remain protected as the **Reserva Extrativista Chico Mendes**. It is possible to visit, staying in comfortable lodge accommodation and seeing both the rubber tappers – who continue their way of life – and abundant wildlife. **Chico Mendes'** house in Xapuri has been preserved as a museum (see previous page).

---

was shot by cattle ranchers Darly Alves da Silva and Darcy Alves Ferreira when he left his back door to go for a pee in his outhouse. There are still blood stains on the door frame. Xapuri has very basic lodging and two restaurants and a huge condom factory – with prophylactics made from rubber harvested in the surrounding forests.

Chico Mendes' rubber-tappers community near Xapuri is still extant, as is the forest he sought to protect – preserved as the **Reserva Extrativista Chico Mendes**. Jaguar, harpy eagle and tapir are still abundant, as are towering Brazil nut and kapok trees. As well as a functioning rubber tapping community, Xapuri is now an ecotourism venture. Chico Mendes' cousin works as a guide. A one- or two-night stay here is a magical experience and well worth undertaking. Book through **Maanaim**, see page 116.

Brasiléia, Assis Brasil and onwards to Bolivia and Peru

The BR-317 is paved all the way to the borders at **Brasiléia**, opposite the Bolivian town of Cobija, and **Assis Brasil**, where the Peruvian, Bolivian and Brazilian frontiers meet and there is an easy crossing to the Peruvian town of **Iñapari**. There is little reason to stop in either town. Brasiléia is a provincial town of a handful of streets. The Bolivian town of **Cobija** is busier as it's a duty-free port – and a good place to pick up electronics bargains. Unless you want to fly, onward transport into Bolivia is poor – the town is roughly 500 km northwest of La Paz and the road is impassable much of the year. Assis is smaller still, and as the bus passes straight through, whisking visitors through emigration and immigration, there is even less of a reason to stop. Neither town has a bank with an ATM (though there are abundant moneychangers and, in Brasiléia, a Banco do Brasil which will change dollars or TCs with a commission heavy enough to make you whince). Both towns have café-restaurants, pharmacies and taxi stands.

Rondônia and Acre listings

For hotel and restaurant price codes and other relevant information, see pages 10-13.

● Where to stay

Porto Velho *p106, map p107*
$$$ Vila Rica, Av Carlos Gomes 1616, T/F069- 3224 3433, www.hotel vilarica.com.br. Tower block hotel with a restaurant, pool and sauna.
$$ Central, R Tenreiro Aranha 2472, T069-2181 2500, www.enter-net.com.br/hcentral. A big, functional, red and white concrete block with friendly staff and plain but well-kept modern a/c rooms with TVs, work desks and fridges and views on the upper floors. Good breakfast, a laundry service and Wi-Fi for free in all rooms and public areas. 2 mins' walk from the a/c shops, restaurants and cinemas of the new Porto Shopping mall.
$$ Líder, R Carlos Gomes 3189 immediately behind the *rodoviária* to the northeast, T069-3225 2727. Boxy but bright rooms which, despite needing a fresh lick of paint, are clean. All come with en suites with solar-heated hot water and breakfast is included.
$$ Por do Sol, R Carlos Gomes 3168 immediately behind the *rodoviária* to the northeast, T069-3222 9161, hotelpordosol @yahoo.com.br. A corridor of peach and brown tile a/c rooms, the best of which have large windows and are in the middle of the corridor. Some have space for 3 people, making this **$** per person. Free Wi-Fi, breakfast included.
$$ Samauma, R Dom Pedro II 1038, T069-3224 5300, hotelsamauma@hotmail.com. Much the best mid-range option in the city centre with brick annexes of cosy, comfortable rooms all with a/c, international TV and en suites gathered around a popular restaurant. Free Wi-Fi in all areas, breakfast and friendly, welcoming staff.
$$-$ Tía Carmen, Av Campos Sales 2995, T069- 3221 7910. Very friendly and with simple well-kept rooms. The snack bar in front of the hotel serves good cakes. There is free Wi-Fi in all rooms.

Guajará-Mirim *p109*
$$$ Pakaas Palafitas Lodge, Km 18, Estrada do Palheta, T/F069-3541 3058, www.pakaas.com.br. 20 mins by taxi from town centre (US$15). 28 smart bungalows in a beautiful natural setting out of town. The hotel is set in forest cut by walking trails and offers canoeing on the river, and has an attractive pool.
$$ Jamaica, Av Leopoldo de Matos 755, T/F069-3541 3721. Simple but the best hotel in town. Rooms have a/c and fridges. Parking.

$$ Lima Palace, Av 15 de Novembro 1613, T069-3541 3421. Similar to the **Jamaica** but with scruffier rooms.

$ Chile, Av Q Bocaiúva. Basic but well run. Includes breakfast, good value but pretty run down.

$ Mamoré, R Mascarenhas de Moraes 1105, T069-3541 3753. Clean, friendly and popular with backpackers.

Rio Branco *p110, map p110*

There are few economical hotels in the centre, but a reasonable selection by the *rodoviária*.

$$$ Imperador Galvez, R Santa Inés 401, T068-3223 7027, www.hotel imperador.com.br. 2 annexes of comfortable, quite modern rooms with international flatscreen TV and free Wi-Fi gathered around a large pool. Breakfasts are enough to last all the way through until the evening.

$$$ Irmãos Inacio Palace, R Rui Barbosa 450-69, T068-3214 7100, www.irmaos pinheiro.com.br. The bright, spacious rooms in this hotel have been refurbished, receiving fresh light peach decor, bathrooms with granite basins and new tiles and functional work desks. The hotel has a pool, free Wi-Fi, serves a generous breakfast and has some English-speaking staff. There's a *churrascaria* restaurant next door.

$$$ Loureiro, R Marechal Deodoro 304, T068-3224 3110. A/c rooms in this freshly refurbished, blocky hotel are scrupulously clean and come with faux-parquet floors, tiled bathrooms and flatscreen TVs. The building is close to the river with many shops and restaurants a stroll away.

$$$ Terra Verde, R Marechal Deodoro 221, T068-3213 6000, www.terraverde hotel.com.br. One of the best in the city with well-appointed a/c rooms and more luxurious Terra Verde suites which come with 2 flatscreens and separate living and sleeping areas. A pool, breakfast and free Wi-Fi throughout.

$$ Afa, R Franco Ribeiro 108, T068-3224 1396. Simple whitewash and wall tile rooms, which, whilst clean, quiet and well-kept, have small windows. Breakfast is generous and there is a very good per kilo lunch restaurant downstairs. Triples are **$** per person.

$$ Papai, R Floriano Peixoto 849, T068-3223 6868. This centrally located hotel has simple but garish pink and lime green a/c rooms the best of which are on the upper floors – those in the basement can be musty. Free Wi-Fi.

$ Ouro Verde, R Uirapuru 326, next to *rodoviária*, T068-3223 2378. This no-frills option has rooms only a little larger than the twin or double beds they contain. But they are clean and set on a long sunny terrace and have plenty of natural light, and each comes with an en suite. Triples work out at **$** per person. With breakfast.

Restaurants

Porto Velho *p106, map p107*

$$$ Caravela do Madeira, R José Camacho 104, Agricolândia, T069-3221 6641. Closed Mon. The best formal restaurant in Porto Velho, in a long wooden dining room perched over the Madeira river. The menu is strong on river fish (the tambaqui is excellent) and the restaurant is one of few in the city to have a wine list.

$$$ Myoshi, Av Amazonas 1280, Bairro NS das Graças, T069-3224 4600, www.myoshi.com.br. This large open-plan dining room serves the best Japanese food in the city with an evening sushi and sashimi buffet. Brazilian fusion options include salmon and cream cheese and sushi tucumã, made with an Amazon river fish. It's a 15-min cab ride from the centre. Also delivers.

$$$-$$ Emporium, Av Presidente Dutra 3366, T069-3221 2665. A very popular restaurant-bar serving hearty portions of river fish, steaks and a wide choice of very cold beer, caipirinhas and juices. The street behind Emporium is known as the Calçada da Fama and is replete with bars and restaurants. It's very busy at weekends.

$$ Café Madeira, Majo Amarantes at Carlos Gomes on the riverfront, T069-3229 1193. The tables perched on a little promontory overlooking the Madeira are a favourite spot for an ice sunset *chopp* draught beer and a *petisco* bar snack. Main courses include steak, river fish and chicken fillets with rice and Brazilian rose coco beans.

Rio Branco *p110, map p110*
There are boats on the river serving cheap but good food. The local specialities are *tacacá*: a soup served piping hot in a gourd, made from *goma* (manioc starch), cooked *jambu* leaves which numb the mouth and tongue, shrimp, spices and hot pepper sauce and a delicious Amazonian take on moqueca, rendered tangy and seet with rainforest herbs and spices.

$$$-$$ Mata Nativa, Estrada Via Verde Km 2 1971, Rio Branco, T069-3221 3004. Regional food served in an open-sided maloca set in a garden on the road to Sena Madureira some 6 km from the centre. Plates are big enough for 4 people and include *moqueca de tambaqui* (Bahian spicy coconut soup with tambaqui fish) and *galinha caipira* (herb-coated chicken served with *pirão* manioc gruel and *vatapa* prawn paste). Very popular on weekends.

$$ Afa, R Franco Ribeiro 108, T069-3224 1396, www.afabistro.com.br. The best and best-value per kilo restaurant in the city, with a wide choice of dishes from tambaqui fish stew, lentils, spit-roast beef, decent.

$$ Elcio, Av Ceará 2513. Superb fish *moquecas* as good as anythign you'll find in Espírito Santo or Bahia in a rich coconut sauce flavoured with an Amazon leaf, *xicoria* and fresh coriander and accompanied with rice, *pirão, farofa* and delicious chilli and *tucupi* sauce. Serves 2-3 people.

O Shopping

Porto Velho *p106, map p107*
Artesanato Indigena Karitiana, R Rui Barbosa 1407 between Jose Camacho and Calama), T069-3229 7591. Daily 0800-1200 and 1400-1700. A Karitiana-run cooperative shop selling indigenous art including beads, earrings and necklaces, ritual items and weapons.

Porto Velho shopping, 2.5 km east of the *rodoviária*, www.pvshopping.com.br. With many a/c boutiques, travel agencies and restaurants in the food emporium and a 6-screen multiplex cinema with films in English.

Markets
There is a clean fruit and veg market at the corner of R Henrique Dias and Av Farquhar and a dry goods market 3 blocks to the south, near the port. On Sun there's a general market off Av Rogério Weber near port, excellent bargains but no souvenirs. Watch out for pickpockets.

▲▲ What to do

Guajará-Mirim *p109*
Alfatur, Av 15 de Novembro 106, T/F069-3541 2853. Tour operator.

Rio Branco *p110, map p110*
Maanaim Amazônia, R Colombia 39, Bairro Bosque, T068-3223 3232, www.maanaim-amazonia.com. One of the best tour operators in the Brazilian Amazon, with a fascinating range of trips, including expeditons to the remote Serra do Divisor National Park, visits to Ashaninka, Yawanawa and other indigenous communities, and stays in the Serengal Cachoeira Chico Mendes rainforest reserve in Xapuri (see page 113).

Porto Velho *p106, map p107*

Air
To get to the airport take bus 'Aeroporto' (last one between 2400 and 0100). Flights to **Brasília**, **Manaus** and **Rio Branco** and other destinations – see page 106.

Boat
See Routes in Amazônia, page 97. There is a regular passenger service from the port – **Porto Cai N'Água** (which means 'fall in the water') up the Madeira to Manaus. For the best price buy directly on the boat, avoid touts on the shore. The Rio Madeira is fairly narrow, so the banks can be seen and there are several 'meetings of waters'.

Bus
Many restaurants and snack bars in the *rodoviária*, 24-hr ATM. Any **Esperança da Communidade** or **Presidente Roosevelt** local bus runs the 1.5 km from the cathedral in the city centre to the *rodoviária*. There are buses to **Campo Grande** (27 hrs, US$155), 2 daily 1st at 0600; **Cuiabá** (24 hrs, US$75), 6 daily; **Guajará-Mirim** (5-6 hrs, US$22) 6 daily from 0630, fastest at midday; **Rio Branco** (8 hrs, US$32), 5 daily; **São Paulo** (40 hrs, US$185), 1 daily at 1000.

Guajará-Mirim *p109*
Bus To **Porto Velho**, 5½ hrs or more depending on season, 8 a day with **Viação Rondônia**, US$18. A taxi to the Porto Velho *rodoviária* costs US$25 per person for 4-5 people, 3 hrs, and leaves when full.

Rio Branco *p110, map p110*
Air For transport to and from the airport see page 112. There are flights to **Porto Velho**, **Manaus**, **Brasília**, **São Paulo**, **Cuiabá** and **Campo Grande** and to **Cruzeiro do Sul**.
Bus To **Porto Velho**, Viação Rondônia, 5

daily, 8-10 hrs, US$50. To **Guajará-Mirim**, daily with **Rondônia** at 1130 and 2200, 8 hrs, US$50; or take **Inácio's Tur** shopping trip, 3 per week.
Car hire Car rentals with nationwide agencies are more expensive in Acre than other states. **Locabem**, Rodovia AC-40, Km 0, 2nd district, T069-3223 3000. **Localiza**, R Rio Grande do Sul 310, T069-3224 7746, airport T069-3224 8478. **Unidas**, T069-3224 5044.

Porto Velho *p106, map p107*
Banks Open until 1400 only. There are numerous **Bradesco** and **HSBC banks** with ATMs in town, including in the airport and at Bradesco, Av 7 de Setembro 711, Centro and HSBC, Av Campos Sales, 2645, Centro.
Laundry Lavanderia Marmoré, Pinheiro Machado 1455B. **Medical services** Hospital Central, R Júlio de Castilho 149, T/F069-3224 4389, 24-hr emergencies. **Dentist** at Carlos Gomes 2577; 24-hr clinic opposite. **Post office** Av Pres Dutra 2701, corner of Av 7 de Setembro. **Telephone** Av Pres Dutra 3023 and Dom Pedro II, daily 0600-2300.

Guajará-Mirim *p109*
Banks Banco do Brasil, foreign exchange in the morning only. **Loja Nogueira**, Av Pres Dutra, corner Leopoldo de Matos, cash only. There is no market in Brazil for bolivianos. **Embassies and consulates** Bolivia, Av C Marquês 495, T069-3541 2862, visas are given here. **Medical services** Regional, Av Mcal Deodoro, T069-3541 2651. **Post office** Av Pres Dutra. **Telephone** Av B Ménzies 751.

Rio Branco *p110, map p110*
Banks There are plenty in town and at the airport, including **Bradesco**, Praça Eurico Dutra 65, T068-3223 2016. **Medical services** Santa Casa hospital, R Alvorada 178, T068-224 6297. **Post office** On the corner of R Epaminondas Jácome and Av Getúlio Vargas.

Contents

Footnotes

Basic Portuguese for travellers

Learning Portuguese is a useful part of the preparation for a trip to Brazil and no volume of dictionaries, phrase books or word lists will provide the same enjoyment as being able to communicate directly with the people of the country you are visiting. It is a good idea to make an effort to grasp the basics before you go. As you travel you will pick up more of the language and the more you know, the more you will benefit from your stay. ▸▸ *See also Language, page 17.*

General pronunciation

Within Brazil itself, there are variations in pronunciation, intonation, phraseology and slang. This makes for great richness and for the possibility of great enjoyment in the language. A couple of points which the newcomer to the language will spot immediately are the use of the tilde (~) over 'a' and 'o'. This makes the vowel nasal, as does a word ending in 'm' or 'ns', or a vowel followed by 'm' + consonant, or by 'n' + consonant. Another important point of spelling is that for words ending in 'i' and 'u' the emphasis is on the last syllable, though (unlike Spanish) no accent is used. This is especially relevant in place names like Buriti, Guarapari, Caxambu, Iguaçu. Note also the use of 'ç', which changes the pronunciation of c from hard [k] to soft [s].

Personal pronouns

In conversation, most people refer to 'you' as *você*, although in the south and in Pará *tu* is more common. To be more polite, use *O Senhor/A Senhora*. For 'us', *gente* (people, folks) is very common when it includes you too.

Portuguese words and phrases

Greetings and courtesies

hello	*oi*
good morning	*bom dia*
good afternoon	*boa tarde*
good evening/night	*boa noite*
goodbye	*adeus/tchau*
see you later	*até logo*
please	*por favor/faz favor*
thank you	*obrigado* (if a man is speaking) */obrigada* (if a woman is speaking)
thank you very much	*muito obrigado/muito obrigada*
how are you?	*como vai você tudo bem?/tudo bom?*
I am fine	*vou bem/tudo bem*
pleased to meet you	*um prazer*
no	*não*
yes	*sim*
excuse me	*com licença*
I don't understand	*não entendo*

please speak slowly	*fale devagar por favor*
what is your name?	*qual é seu nome?*
my name is …	*o meu nome é …*
go away!	*vai embora!*

Basic questions

where is?	*onde está/onde fica?*
why?	*por que?*
how much does it cost?	*quanto custa?*
what for?	*para que?*
how much is it?	*quanto é?*
how do I get to … ?	*para chegar a … ?*
when?	*quando?*
I want to go to …	*quero ir para …*
when does the bus leave?/arrive?	*a que hor sai/chega o ônibus?*
is this the way to the church?	*aquí é o caminho para a igreja?*

Basics

bathroom/toilet	*banheiro*
police (policeman)	*a polícia (o polícia)*
hotel	*o (a pensão, a hospedaria)*
restaurant	*o restaurante (o lanchonete)*
post office	*o correio*
telephone office	*(central) telefônica*
supermarket	*o supermercado*
market	*o mercado*
bank	*o banco*
bureau de change	*a casa de câmbio*
exchange rate	*a taxa de câmbio*
notes/coins	*notas/moedas*
traveller's cheques	*os travelers/os cheques de viagem*
cash	*dinheiro*
breakfast	*o caféde manh*
lunch	*o almoço*
dinner/supper	*o jantar*
Meal	*a refeição*
drink	*a bebida*
mineral water	*a água mineral*
soft fizzy drink	*o refrigerante*
beer	*a cerveja*
without sugar	*sem açúcar*
without meat	*sem carne*

Getting around

on the left/right	*à esquerda/à direita*
straight on	*direto*

to walk	*caminhar*
bus station	*a rodoviária*
bus	*o ônibus*
bus stop	*a parada*
train	*a trem*
airport	*o aeroport*
aeroplane/airplane	*o avião*
flight	*o vôa*
first/second class	*primeira/segunda clase*
train station	*a ferroviária*
combined bus and train station	*a rodoferroviária*
ticket	*o passagem/o bilhete*
ticket office	*a bilheteria*

Accommodation

room	*quarto*
noisy	*barulhento*
single/double room	*(quarto de) solteiro/(quarto para) casal*
room with two beds	*quarto com duas camas*
with private bathroom	*quarto com banheiro*
hot/cold water	*água quente/fria*
to make up/clean	*limpar*
sheet(s)	*o lençol (os lençóis)*
blankets	*as mantas*
pillow	*o travesseiro*
clean/dirty towels	*as toalhas limpas/sujas*
toilet paper	*o papel higiêico*

Health

chemist	*a farmacia*
doctor	*o coutor/a doutora*
(for) pain	*(para) dor*
stomach	*o esômago (a barriga)*
head	*a cabeça*
fever/sweat	*a febre/o suor higiênicas*
diarrhoea	*a diarréia*
blood	*o sangue*
condoms	*as camisinhas/os preservativos*
contraceptive (pill)	*anticonceptional (a pílula)*
period	*a menstruação/a regra*
sanitary towels/tampons	*toalhas absorventes/absorventes internos*
contact lenses	*lentes de contacto*

Time

at one o'clock (am/pm)	*a uma hota (da manhã/da tarde)*
at half past two/two thirty	*as dois e meia*

at a quarter to three	*quinze para as três*
it's one o'clock	*é uma*
it's seven o'clock	*são sete horas*
it's twenty past six/six twenty	*são seis e vinte*
it's five to nine	*são cinco para as nove*
in ten minutes	*em dez minutos*
five hours	*cinco horas*
does it take long?	*sura muito?*

Days

Monday	*segunda feiro*
Tuesday	*terça feira*
Wednesday	*quarta feira*
Thursday	*quinta feira*
Friday	*sexta feira*
Saturday	*sábado*
Sunday	*domingo*

Months

January	*janeiro*
February	*fevereiro*
March	*março*
April	*abril*
May	*maio*
June	*junho*
July	*julho*
August	*agosto*
September	*setembro*
October	*outubro*
November	*novembro*
December	*dezembro*

Numbers

one	*um/uma*
two	*dois/duas*
three	*três*
four	*quatro*
five	*cinco*
six	*seis* ('*meia*' half, is frequently used for number 6 ie half-dozen)
seven	*sete*
eight	*oito*
nine	nove
ten	*dez*
eleven	*onze*
twelve	*doze*

thirteen	*treze*
fourteen	*catorze*
fifteen	*quinze*
sixteen	*dezesseis*
seventeen	*dezessete*
eighteen	*dezoito*
nineteen	*dezenove*
twenty	*vinte*
twenty-one	*vente e um*
thirty	*trinta*
forty	*cuarenta*
fifty	*cinqüe*
sixty	*sessenta*
seventy	*setenta*
eighty	*oitenta*
ninety	*noventa*
hundred	*cem, cento*
thousand	*mil*

Useful slang

that's great/cool	*que legal*
bloke/guy/geezer	*cara* (literally 'face')
biker slang for bloke/guy	*mano*
cheesy/tacky	*brega*
posh, spoilt girl/boy with rich parents	*patricinha/mauricinho*
in fashion/cool	*descolado*

Glossary

azulejo	tile	*fazenda*	country estate or ranch
baía	bay	*feijoada*	black-bean stew
bairro	area or suburb	*ferroviária*	train station
bandas	marching bands that compete during Carnaval	*forró*	music and dance style from northeast Brazil
bandeirantes	early Brazilian conquistadors who went on missions to open	*frevo*	frenetic musical style from Recife
	up the interior	*gaúcho*	cowboy, especially from Rio Grande do Sul
barraca	beach hut or stall	*garimpeiro*	miner or prospector
berimbau	stringed instrument that accompanies capoeira	*igreja*	church
		ilha	island
biblioteca	library	*jangada*	small fishing boats, peculiar to the northeast
bilhete	ticket		
botequim	small bar, open-air	*jardim*	garden
caboclo	rural workers of mixed descent	*lanchonete*	café/deli
cachaça	cane liquor	*largo*	small square
cachoeira	waterfall	*leito*	executive bus
caipirinha	Brazilian cocktail, made from *cachaça*, lime, sugar and ice	*litoral*	coast/coastal area
		mata	jungle
câmbio	bureau de change	*mercado*	market
candomblé	African-Brazilian religion	*Mineiro*	person from Minas Gerais
capela	chapel	*mirante*	viewpoint
capoeira	African-Brazilian martial art	*mosteiro*	monastery
Carioca	person from Rio de Janeiro	*Paulista*	person from São Paulo
carnaval	carnival	*ponte*	bridge
cerrado	scubland	*praça*	square/plaza
cerveja	beer	*praia*	beach
churrascaria	barbecue restaurant, often all-you-can-eat	*prancha*	surfboard
		prefeitura	town hall
empadas	mini pasties	*rio*	river
estrada	road	*rodoviária*	bus station
favela	slum/shanty town	*rua*	street

Acronyms and official names

FUNAI	Fundacao Nacional do Indio (National Foundation for Indigenous People)
IBAMA	Instituto Brasileiro do Meio Ambiente E Dos Recursos Naturais Renováveis (Brazilian Institute of Environment and Renewable Natural Resources)
MPB	Música Popular Brasileira
RAMSAR	Wetlands Convention

Index

Titles available in the Footprint *Focus* range

Latin America	UK RRP	US RRP
Bahia & Salvador	£7.99	$11.95
Brazilian Amazon	£7.99	$11.95
Brazilian Pantanal	£6.99	$9.95
Buenos Aires & Pampas	£7.99	$11.95
Cartagena & Caribbean Coast	£7.99	$11.95
Costa Rica	£8.99	$12.95
Cuzco, La Paz & Lake Titicaca	£8.99	$12.95
El Salvador	£5.99	$8.95
Guadalajara & Pacific Coast	£6.99	$9.95
Guatemala	£8.99	$12.95
Guyana, Guyane & Suriname	£5.99	$8.95
Havana	£6.99	$9.95
Honduras	£7.99	$11.95
Nicaragua	£7.99	$11.95
Northeast Argentina & Uruguay	£8.99	$12.95
Paraguay	£5.99	$8.95
Quito & Galápagos Islands	£7.99	$11.95
Recife & Northeast Brazil	£7.99	$11.95
Rio de Janeiro	£8.99	$12.95
São Paulo	£5.99	$8.95
Uruguay	£6.99	$9.95
Venezuela	£8.99	$12.95
Yucatán Peninsula	£6.99	$9.95

Asia	UK RRP	US RRP
Angkor Wat	£5.99	$8.95
Bali & Lombok	£8.99	$12.95
Chennai & Tamil Nadu	£8.99	$12.95
Chiang Mai & Northern Thailand	£7.99	$11.95
Goa	£6.99	$9.95
Gulf of Thailand	£8.99	$12.95
Hanoi & Northern Vietnam	£8.99	$12.95
Ho Chi Minh City & Mekong Delta	£7.99	$11.95
Java	£7.99	$11.95
Kerala	£7.99	$11.95
Kolkata & West Bengal	£5.99	$8.95
Mumbai & Gujarat	£8.99	$12.95

For the latest books, e-books and a wealth of travel information, visit us at: www.footprinttravelguides.com.

 footprinttravelguides.com

Africa & Middle East	UK RRP	US RRP
Beirut	£6.99	$9.95
Cairo & Nile Delta	£8.99	$12.95
Damascus	£5.99	$8.95
Durban & KwaZulu Natal	£8.99	$12.95
Fès & Northern Morocco	£8.99	$12.95
Jerusalem	£8.99	$12.95
Johannesburg & Kruger National Park	£7.99	$11.95
Kenya's Beaches	£8.99	$12.95
Kilimanjaro & Northern Tanzania	£8.99	$12.95
Luxor to Aswan	£8.99	$12.95
Nairobi & Rift Valley	£7.99	$11.95
Red Sea & Sinai	£7.99	$11.95
Zanzibar & Pemba	£7.99	$11.95

Europe	UK RRP	US RRP
Bilbao & Basque Region	£6.99	$9.95
Brittany West Coast	£7.99	$11.95
Cádiz & Costa de la Luz	£6.99	$9.95
Granada & Sierra Nevada	£6.99	$9.95
Languedoc: Carcassonne to Montpellier	£7.99	$11.95
Málaga	£5.99	$8.95
Marseille & Western Provence	£7.99	$11.95
Orkney & Shetland Islands	£5.99	$8.95
Santander & Picos de Europa	£7.99	$11.95
Sardinia: Alghero & the North	£7.99	$11.95
Sardinia: Cagliari & the South	£7.99	$11.95
Seville	£5.99	$8.95
Sicily: Palermo & the Northwest	£7.99	$11.95
Sicily: Catania & the Southeast	£7.99	$11.95
Siena & Southern Tuscany	£7.99	$11.95
Sorrento, Capri & Amalfi Coast	£6.99	$9.95
Skye & Outer Hebrides	£6.99	$9.95
Verona & Lake Garda	£7.99	$11.95

North America	UK RRP	US RRP
Vancouver & Rockies	£8.99	$12.95

Australasia	UK RRP	US RRP
Brisbane & Queensland	£8.99	$12.95
Perth	£7.99	$11.95

 Join us on facebook for the latest travel news, product releases, offers and amazing competitions: www.facebook.com/footprintbooks.